Realist Constructivism

Rethinking International Relations Theory

Realism and constructivism, two key contemporary theoretical approaches to the study of international relations, are commonly taught as mutually exclusive ways of understanding the subject. *Realist Constructivism* explores the common ground between the two, and demonstrates that, rather than being in simple opposition, they have areas of both tension and overlap. There is indeed space to engage in a realist constructivism. But at the same time, there are important distinctions between them, and there remains a need for a constructivism that is not realist, and a realism that is not constructivist. Samuel Barkin argues more broadly for a different way of thinking about theories of international relations, that focuses on the corresponding elements within various approaches rather than on a small set of mutually exclusive paradigms. *Realist Constructivism* provides an interesting new way for scholars and students to think about international relations theory.

J. SAMUEL BARKIN is Associate Professor of Political Science at the University of Florida. His previous books include *International Organization: Theories and Institutions* (2006) and *Social Construction and the Logic of Money* (2003). He was also the co-editor of *Anarchy and the Environment* (1999).

Realist Constructivism

SAMUEL BARKIN

Department of Political Science
University of Florida

CAMBRIDGE
UNIVERSITY PRESS

CAMBRIDGE UNIVERSITY PRESS
Cambridge, New York, Melbourne, Madrid, Cape Town, Singapore,
São Paulo, Delhi, Tokyo, Mexico City

Cambridge University Press
The Edinburgh Building, Cambridge CB2 8RU, UK

Published in the United States of America by Cambridge University Press,
New York

www.cambridge.org
Information on this title: www.cambridge.org/9780521198714

First published 2010
Reprinted 2011

Printed in the United Kingdom at the University Press, Cambridge

A catalogue record for this publication is available from the British Library

Library of Congress Cataloguing in Publication data
Barkin, J. Samuel, 1965–
    Realist constructivism : rethinking international relations theory / J. Samuel Barkin.
    p.   cm.
    ISBN 978-0-521-19871-4 (hardback)
    1. International relations.   2. Constructive realism.   I. Title.
    JZ1242.B38 2010
    327.101–dc22
    2009053425

ISBN 978-0-521-19871-4 Hardback
ISBN 978-0-521-12181-1 Paperback

Contents

Acknowledgements

About a decade ago, I began to get frustrated with the common assumption that the relationship between constructivism and realism was one of mutual opposition, and that there was little ground for a useful conversation between the two. It struck me that the two approaches are based on assumptions that are orthogonal to, rather than contradictory of, each other. Furthermore, it struck me that a conversation between the two could serve as a useful model for examining the relationships among approaches to international relations theory understood as concepts rather than as paradigms. I tried out these ideas on my graduate students, along with my colleagues, and they recommended that I write up this set of ideas. I began with an article-length manuscript making the first stage of the argument, that realism and constructivism are not incompatible.

Early signs that this argument would find an audience were not promising. The manuscript was rejected by five journals. Most of the reviews suggested that the argument just wasn't interesting, that nobody would read it. A few of the reviews took great umbrage at the argument, either because it suggested that realism should be watered down with constructivism, or because it suggested that constructivism might be sullied by realism. Eventually (in 2003) the manuscript found a home at *International Studies Review*, and I was pleasantly surprised to find a community with which it resonated. Many other scholars, it turns out, had been thinking along similar lines, and many of these scholars have been both helpful and supportive in the process of writing this book.

The idea of writing the book began to develop in a workshop on realism and constructivism organized by Patrick Jackson and Daniel Nexon, held at Georgetown University in 2005. Patrick and Dan had organized a forum on realist constructivism the previous year, also in *International Studies Review*, with contributions from Janice Bially Mattern, Richard Ned Lebow, and Jennifer Sterling-Folker, as well as Patrick and Dan and me. The enthusiasm of this group for this project has provided key encouragement. Others who have provided both encouragement and feedback include Stefano Guzzini and Ido Oren, both of whom have written seminal work on the limits of contemporary realism. Thanks are also due to Peg Hermann, who edited *International Studies Review* at the time, and who made the decision to publish both the original realist constructivism article and the forum the next year, as well as to Bruce Cronin, David Ellis, Audie Klotz, Chris Layne, and all of the participants at the Georgetown seminar and at a seminar in the University of Florida's Political Science Department in 2008 at which this research was presented.

Thanks particularly are due to Janice Bially Mattern and Jennifer Sterling-Folker, who both read complete drafts of the book manuscript and provided invaluable feedback and advice. And to John Haslam of Cambridge University Press, as well as two anonymous reviewers who provided detailed and excellent comments. Research assistance was provided by Kuniyuki Nishimura (who also read and commented on the entire draft) and Sean Walsh. The index was compiled by Ty Solomon. My greatest debt of gratitude goes to Beth DeSombre, who not only provided comments on the complete manuscript, but also provided encouragement and feedback throughout the life of the project.

Finally, an acknowledgement of those institutions that supported me during the writing of this book. The University of Florida provided the sabbatical that allowed the book to be written, and provides a wonderfully collegial Political Science Department when I am not on sabbatical. Debbie Wallen and Sue Lawless-Yanchisin have both given administrative (and moral) support over the years far beyond the call of duty. While on sabbatical I was hosted by Brown University's Watson Institute for International Studies (thanks to Peter Andreas for suggesting and Tom Biersteker for formalizing my stay there) and Harvard University's Olin Institute for Security Studies (thanks to Steven Rosen).

Portions of the text of this book have appeared previously in two articles. Parts of Chapters 6 and 8 appear as "Realism, Prediction, and Foreign Policy" in *Foreign Policy Analysis* 5: 3 (July 2009), and parts of "Realist Constructivism," originally published in *International Studies Review* 5: 3 (September 2003, pp. 325–342), are scattered throughout the book.

1 | Introduction

In the sociology of science, paradigms are a bit like castles.[1] Scientists are knights in this metaphor, and assumptions are the liege-lords that the knights/scientists are sworn to defend. The strength of a paradigm can be measured by how many scientists are willing to defend its ramparts. Scientists tend to retain allegiance to their assumptions, so that the paradigmatic castles defend their inhabitants successfully, until those inhabitants die off. In this metaphor, it is in the nature of paradigms to be mutually exclusive – as a knight/scientist, one is more concerned about defending one's castle/paradigm, and in defeating others, than in building bridges among them. Paradigms, in other words, are distinct from, and in opposition to, each other.

This view of paradigms has been regularly co-opted in discussing both the sociology and the epistemology of international relations as a discipline. Thomas Kuhn's seminal discussion of paradigms and the sociology of science is regularly taught in graduate international relations theory courses, despite Kuhn's suggestions that his argument does not necessarily apply to social science.[2] Whether or not one accepts Kuhn's argument about the sociology of the natural sciences, and whether or not one sees paradigms in the social sciences as being equivalent to those in the natural sciences, it remains the case that the language of paradigms pervades thinking about international relations theory.[3] And with this thinking comes the castle mentality, in which paradigms are seen as mutually exclusive, as distinct ways of looking at international politics that should be kept separate, as things to be defended against other paradigms.

---

[1] The term 'paradigm' is used here following Kuhn 1970.
[2] For example Kuhn 1991.
[3] See, for example, Maliniak *et al.* 2007, which is in large part built around paradigms.

The core argument of this book is that this paradigmatic way of thinking about different approaches to the study of international relations is problematic. It obscures both the compatibilities among different approaches, and the complex ways in which they interrelate. In building paradigmatic castles, it encourages insular thinking, and a focus on emphasizing differences. It also encourages paradigmatic partisans to try to fit too much within the walls of their particular approach, in an attempt to make their paradigmatic castle self-sufficient. In this way, it encourages what might be called a paradigmatic imperialism at the expense of communication within the discipline. Two particular approaches to the study of international relations that are often identified as paradigms are constructivism and realism, and the focus of this book is on the various relationships (ontological, epistemological, and political) between the two.

Constructivism and realism appear to have taken their places in the literature on international relations theory in direct opposition to each other. Examples of this opposition can be found in a number of places. Self-proclaimed constructivists often have (or at least are seen to have) worldviews that fall within liberalism, broadly defined, and often accept that categorization.[4] Moreover, some constructivist theorizing argues explicitly that constructivism and realism are logically incompatible[5] or, at least, antagonistic.[6] International relations pedagogy is also increasingly defining realism and constructivism as being categorically distinct, as witnessed by the increasing tendency in IR textbooks, even at the introductory level, to define realism and constructivism as two of three or more distinct paradigms in the field.[7] And constructivist theory came into the IR mainstream as a critique of structural or neorealism.[8] While much of this critique was specific to neorealism, and as such does not apply to classical realism, it set the tone for the incommensurability of constructivism with realism more generally.

To claim that constructivism is an IR paradigm equivalent to realism or liberalism is misleading, and the tendency to do so in textbooks is rarely mirrored in the scholarly literature. In the latter, constructivism

[4] Barkin 2003a.
[5] For example, Wendt 1999; Patomäki and Wight 2000.
[6] Lebow 2001.
[7] For example, Hughes 2000; Kegley and Wittkopf 2001; Lieber 2001.
   See also Maliniak *et al.* 2007.
[8] Wendt 1987; Dessler 1989; Onuf and Klink 1989.

is usually identified as an ontology, epistemology, or methodology. But even here, the castle mindset is in evidence. Constructivism is usually defined as being distinct from either materialism or rationalism, with a wall separating social construction on the one hand from a materialist or rationalist mindset on the other. A prominent state-of-the-field exercise, in fact, identified the rationalism–constructivism controversy as the central debate in contemporary IR theory.[9] Constructivists who claim their methodology is incompatible with realism focus on the association between realism and both materialism and rationalism. Realists who claim their paradigm is incompatible with constructivism focus for the most part not on the methodology *per se* but on a perceived tendency for constructivists to be idealists or utopians.

Neither argument, however, holds up to careful scrutiny. Claims by constructivists that realist theory is incompatible with intersubjective epistemologies and methodologies are based on either caricatures or very narrow understandings of realism. And realist critics of constructivism are similarly guilty of inferring from the worldviews of some (perhaps many) practicing constructivists that the methodology is inherently biased toward liberalism. An examination of constructivist epistemology and classical realist theory suggests that they are, in fact, compatible. Not, of course, that good constructivism is necessarily realist, or that good realism is necessarily constructivist. But rather that constructivist research is as compatible with a realist worldview as with any other (and more compatible with realism than with some), and that the realist worldview in turn can benefit from constructivist research methods.

A realist/constructivist synthesis would in particular serve a number of useful functions as part of the geography of international relations theory. One is to clear up a number of debates in the field in which the protagonists speak past, rather than to, each other, particularly with respect to the definition of, and relationships among, various approaches. Another is a language with which to speak to the relationship between the study of power politics and the study of ideals in international relations on the one hand, and the study of the social construction of international politics on the other. A third function is to clarify the relationships between mainstream approaches to

---

[9] Katzenstein, Keohane, and Krasner 1998; Ruggie 1998. See also Keohane 1988 and Fearon and Wendt 2002.

international relations and critical and postmodern approaches that view both constructivism and realism with skepticism, albeit for different reasons. A final function, perhaps the most useful for both realist and constructivist scholars of international politics, is to clarify both the core concepts and limitations of these two approaches themselves.

From paradigms to realist/constructivist synthesis

To get to a discussion of the specific relationships between constructivism and realism requires four steps. The first is a critique of what might be called paradigmatism, an understanding of the discipline of international relations as a set of discrete paradigms that need not interact, that need not inform each other. What we tend to think of as paradigms cannot successfully serve the function of complete sets of assumptions that suffice as starting points for research into international politics, for two reasons. The first is that each of these so-called paradigms is really an assumption about one particular aspect of the study of international relations. In the case of constructivism, this aspect is sociological, the assumption that we can usefully understand political institutions as social constructs. In the case of realism, this aspect is political, the assumption that power will remain a salient feature of politics, whatever the institutional structure. The former tells us about how to study politics, but little about how politics work. The latter tells us about how politics work, but not how to study them.[10]

To think in terms of paradigms, then, is to jumble together assumptions about epistemology, methodology, politics, and a variety of other things. Realist political theory tells us little about methodology. To think in terms of a realist paradigm, then, is to underspecify method in the study of international politics. Analogically, constructivist epistemology tells us little about politics *per se*, and thus to think in terms of a constructivist paradigm is to underspecify political theory. Any study of actual political practice requires both method and a theory of politics. Focusing on particular paradigms, therefore, does not give us a sufficiently broad set of assumptions, of background conditions, for actual research into international relations.

What can happen as a result is that paradigms expand to fill in the missing assumptions. But since the expansion is beyond the scope of

[10] Jervis 1998 makes this point.

the original focus of the paradigm, the new assumptions are often not grounded in the same logic as the original core assumptions of the paradigm. This expansion can have various effects, some benign, some pernicious. In the case of constructivism, the process of expansion often leads in the context of specific research projects either to the unreflexive adoption of political theory in a way that is incompatible with the basic tenets of the approach, or to a focus on social theorizing for its own sake that distracts from rather than illuminates the study of international politics.

In the case of realism, the effects of paradigmatic expansion are even more problematic. The attempt over the past four decades to make realism more "scientific" by trying to make it into a predictive tool in the manner of the behavioralist approach to social science has not only served to distract from the core realist insights about power and politics, but has actively undermined realism's ability to pursue those insights. This distraction is particularly true of neorealism, and in fact I make the argument that neorealism, in attempting to make a systemic theory out of realism, has lost sight of the key insights of the approach.[11] Whatever one thinks of neorealism in its own terms, it is in this sense a failure as an attempt to systematize realism. The realism that is presented in this book as compatible with constructivism is the classical version, and the various discussions of realism here should be read in that light.

These observations lead to the second step in getting to the discussion of constructivism and realism, which is the claim that the discipline is better served by thinking of the various approaches to the study of international relations in terms of core concepts rather than in terms of paradigms. The core concepts underlying constructivism and realism, I will argue, are intersubjectivity and power politics respectively. The key differences between core concepts and paradigms are twofold. The first lies in the process of definition. Paradigms are an all-encompassing way of looking at the world in the context of a particular discipline or object of study.[12] As such, thinking of

---

[11] Archetypical works of classical realism, as I use the term, include: Morgenthau 1948; Carr 1964; Wolfers 1962. Archetypical works of neorealism include: Waltz 1979; Gilpin 1981; Mearsheimer 2001. For discussions of the process of getting from one to the other, see *inter alia* Jervis 1994 and Guzzini 1998.
[12] For example, Kuhn 1970, p. 175.

approaches as paradigms can lead to maximalist definitions, in which the paradigm is seen to speak to all aspects of study. Core concepts, conversely, lend themselves to minimalist definitions, and the acceptance that many aspects of a particular study will be orthogonal to the concept. Only by stripping down definitions of the approaches to these core concepts can we recover something that is about the study of international politics, rather than the disciplinary politics of international relations.

The second key difference between core concepts and paradigms is the way in which they interact. Paradigms stand in opposition to each other: to believe in one is to reject others. This leaves little ground for thinking of ways in which they relate to each other. Concepts interact in more complicated ways. Sometimes they are orthogonal to each other. Sometimes they do in fact have a relationship of opposition, but even then the relationship will not necessarily follow the exclusionary pattern of paradigmatic thinking. For example, realism clearly defines itself in opposition to idealism. But this opposition is dialectic rather than exclusionary – the seminal realists of the middle of the twentieth century recognized that realist logic was meaningless in the absence of political idealism, even as they argued against a politics based on that idealism.

Which in turn leads to the third step in getting to a discussion of constructivism and realism: the observation that the core concepts underlying the various approaches to the study of international relations interact in various and complex ways. There is of course a trade-off in looking at these interactions. Without some attempt to categorize or to order them, understanding the interaction among approaches becomes difficult, as there is no conceptual framework for communication among practitioners of the various approaches. Conversely, too simplified or rigid a categorization can stifle communication by failing to recognize the various links among approaches. The paradigmatic view is in a way the ultimate in simplistic categorizations, in that it labels a given piece of research as either in or out of the paradigm. Somewhere between a rigidly paradigmatic approach and an unordered conceptual free-for-all is a level of categorization that is amenable to productive communication among approaches.

One way to look at this middle ground is to see disciplinary approaches in a grid, or a matrix. In this view, the core propositions of an approach speak to some dimensions of the study of international relations, but not to others. These dimensions can be methodological, epistemological, political, or a variety of other things. Realism, in this view, would take a clear position in the dimension of the place of power politics in the study of international relations, but would not speak clearly to various specifically methodological questions. Constructivism would take a much clearer position on questions of the ontological relationship between individual and society than on questions of the role of power in society. Pairs of approaches could then be related in the matrix as compatible on some dimensions, incompatible on others, and, quite often, orthogonal on many. This matrix need not be formalized, and is perhaps best not formalized. A matrix with an indeterminate number of dimensions will be more flexible in encouraging communications between various approaches, defined in various ways, but at the same time gives a framework for seeing approaches in the broader context of the discipline, and of conceptual relationships within the discipline.

Using this matrix metaphor as a lens provides the fourth step in getting to a discussion of constructivism and realism. This lens gives us a way to look at the relationship between the two approaches, that allows us to see points of tangent, points of opposition, and dimensions in which the two approaches are orthogonal. A realist/ constructivist synthesis can then be built around the points of tangent, in which the two approaches reinforce each other where they are orthogonal, that is nonetheless cognizant of the real points of tension between them. Most of this book is devoted to the application of this lens to this particular relationship. It looks at a variety of dimensions on which the two approaches are compatible or in tension, as well as dimensions on which one is clearly located but the other is not. It also looks at dimensions on which the conventional wisdom sees the two in tension, but upon closer examination this tension turns out to be false. This is particularly true of the purported tension between materialism and ideas, and that between social construction and rationality.

The resulting synthesis is one that brings from classical realism a focus on power politics and on foreign policy, and from constructivism a focus on, and a methodology for studying, the co-constitution of structures and agents. It builds on a common foundation of a logic of the social, and a demand for reflexivity and historical context found in both constructivism and classical realism. It is very much not the stuff of a new paradigm – being a hybrid, it suffers the limitations of both constructivism and realism, and as such is only applicable to a subset of questions in international relations, those that look at the social construction of public policy, particularly foreign policy, in international politics. But within the context of that subset of questions, it can usefully inform the work of both constructivists and realists.

This sense of limitation distinguishes the argument being made here from those made in earlier discussions of a realist/constructivist synthesis, such as Michael Williams' *The Realist Tradition and the Limits of International Relations* and Roger Spegele's *Political Realism in International Theory*.[13] The synthesis in these works is often for the purpose of what might be called a rehabilitation of classical realism. Constructivism plays the role of providing epistemological and ontological heft to classical realist insights about morality and prudence in international politics. As such, constructivism is used in these works to the end of reinforcing a realist paradigm that avoids the internal contradictions of neorealism, and of the positivist turn of contemporary realism more generally. These works are, in other words, exercises in paradigm building. While clearly sympathetic to a rehabilitation of classical realism, I argue against paradigm building. This book proposes the non-paradigmatic interaction of approaches to the study of international relations, rather than an argument for a new paradigm, inasmuch as it addresses the limitations as much as the possibilities of a synthesis of constructivism and realism, and contextualizes the synthesis in the broader geography of the field.

Plan of the book

While these four steps describe the overall logic of this book, they do not describe the order of presentation of the argument. Rather, the book proceeds by looking sequentially at various dimensions of international relations theory that are relevant to the creation of a synthesis of realist constructivism. It attempts to build the relevant part of the matrix, and to draw from it observations both on constructivism and realism individually, their internal logics and their relationships with other approaches to the study of international relations, and on the relationship between the two.

[13] Williams 2005; Spegele 1996.

A first step in this process is the definition of terms, particularly definitions of constructivism and realism. As noted above, the operational definition of constructivism that I propose centers on intersubjectivity, whereas that of realism centers on power politics. Both definitions are somewhat contentious, the latter probably more so than the former. Chapter 2 is therefore devoted to unpacking, explaining, and justifying these definitions. In the case of realism, it argues that the various definitional elements that have often been proposed for realism all stem from the assumption that power politics matters. Focusing on power politics obviates the need for these additional elements. It also focuses attention on the core realist proposition that not only is power politics present in international relations, but it is central to them. In the case of constructivism, it argues that defining the approach in negative terms, of things that it is opposed to, is less useful than defining it in positive terms that give the scholar guidance on what to do, rather than on what not to do. Furthermore, the oppositional concepts most often used, materialism and rationalism, are problematic. The following two chapters discuss why.

Materialism is the focus of Chapter 3. This chapter does four things. First, it looks at the ideas/materialism dichotomy, and finds that it is not quite as dichotomous as many make it out to be. There are few scholars out there who deny that there are ideas embedded in our material reality, and to make the argument that realists are at heart brute materialists is to create a rhetorical straw man. Second, it looks at the ideas/materialism distinction in the context of international relations theory more broadly, and finds that the distance between constructivism and realism on this issue may in fact be less than the distance between constructivism and many variants of both Marxism and liberalism. And finally, it makes the case that the real distinction that proponents of an ideas/materialism dichotomy are getting at is really about history rather than materiality. This dichotomy is really between approaches that look primarily to historical context and those that understand social institutions as transhistorical in nature.

Chapter 4 examines the distinction between rationalist and sociological approaches to international relations theory. This distinction is a tricky one. There is certainly a fundamental ontological difference between the methodologically individualist approach to social science underlying rationalism, and the methodological holism underlying sociological approaches. But this does not mean that the former can look only at strategic behavior, and the latter only at appropriate behavior. Furthermore, this difference is largely irrelevant to a discussion of the relationship between constructivism and realism, because neither of these approaches is methodologically individualist. Classical realism speaks of rationality, but uses the term in a different way than does, say, rational choice theory. Realism is in fact more on the holistic end of the spectrum, to the extent that its key unit of analysis, the state, is a social aggregate. Its logic is therefore based on the assumption that people will act in the interests of the social aggregate, even when this requires action that is not in their immediate individual self-interest. As such, realism shares with constructivism a foundation in a logic of the social rather than a logic of the individual.

This logic of the social has a number of ramifications, which are the subject of the subsequent two chapters. Chapter 5 looks at the relationship between a logic of the social and the idea of a public, or national, interest. This is a point at which constructivism and realism tangent in interesting ways – both approaches assume the existence of a public interest, but do so in different ways. And in doing so, both distinguish themselves from critical and postmodern approaches that have quite different logics of the social. Chapter 6, meanwhile, discusses the constraints that the aspects of the logic of the social that the two approaches share in common place on both constructivist and realist analysis. The key constraint in this context is reflexivity. Since the logic of the social underlying both approaches assumes that political morality is contextual, scholars in both traditions need to recognize that political activity will be seen elsewhere through a different normative lens than by those who undertake it. Recognizing that this is the case therefore requires of scholars that they examine critically the extent to which their own political morality is embedded in their analysis. Many contemporary realists, particularly neorealists, and probably some constructivists as well, might find this claim to be contentious at best. But it nonetheless inheres in the logics of both classical realism and of constructivism.

The discussion of the logic of the social in these two chapters is primarily about structure, about the ways in which existing social structures both constrain and enable political behavior. But both constructivism and realism look to agency as a, perhaps the, key mechanism for change in these structures, and hence in international politics more generally. Chapter 7 deals with agency in this context, and particularly with the tension between the need for human agency to keep both approaches from being structurally deterministic, and the difficulty faced by both in creating a theory of agency. In fact, I argue that, within the logical constraints of both approaches (and using a fairly narrow definition of agency) one cannot reasonably theorize agency. Thus agency plays the role in these approaches of being at the same time the motor of change, and the conceptual element that prevents both constructivism and realism from being effectively predictive.

The tension between the logic of the social and these constraints on theorizing agency help to define the limits of both constructivism and realism as approaches to studying international relations, and these limits are the subject of the antepenultimate and penultimate chapters. The key practical limit for realism, as argued in Chapter 8, is that the approach cannot succeed in both predicting and prescribing foreign policy. A realism that takes the concept of power seriously cannot reasonably pretend to be able to accurately predict outcomes. And if one does not take power seriously, then one can question the extent to which it is really realist. In other words, realism is at its core a theory of foreign policy, and the attempt to make it into a systemic theory of international politics not only fails to achieve the latter, but undermines the former as well. The key practical limit for constructivism, as noted in Chapter 9, is its inability to frame a general theory of how international politics work. Because the social construction of politics is a function of agency in a particular time and place, the process is particular to that time and place. In other words, constructivism can help us to understand how a particular politics is constructed, but it is much more limited in its ability to help us understand how politics in general is constructed.

The concluding chapter does two things. First, it summarizes the various dimensions of international relations theory discussed in the book, in terms of how these dimensions relate to each other, where both realism and constructivism fit on them, and what this says both about how each of the two fits into the broader conceptual geography of the field, and about the relationship between the two. Then it builds on these observations to offer some thoughts on what a realist/constructivist synthesis might look like, and what it might be well-placed to accomplish. In particular, it discusses how realist insights about power and constructivist method might combine to provide a more robust tool for studying foreign policy than either is capable of alone.

Implicit in these arguments is a broader point about the study of international relations, that a paradigm-centered approach to the discipline hinders our ability to understand international politics more than it helps. A realist/constructivist synthesis is but one of many potentially useful combinations of approaches that become available when those approaches are seen as concepts rather than as paradigms. Seeing these approaches as interrelating parts of a matrix, rather than as independent castles, allows international relations scholars to use them effectively to address the questions at hand, rather than trying to fit the various shapes of these questions into the same square paradigm. Seeing these approaches in this way will also help scholars to recognize that no single paradigm provides all of the tools necessary for the study of international relations.

2 | *Definitions*

The first step in a discussion of the relationship between constructivism and realism is defining the two terms as they are used in this book. This is a key step, because debates across paradigmatic lines are often characterized by participants talking past each other, rather than communicating effectively. Part of the reason that scholars engaged in these debates so often talk past each other has to do with the nature of paradigmatic debate, which encourages neither reading nor constructively engaging the work of those working in different paradigms. The defense of paradigmatic castles is not the best starting point for an open exchange of ideas about the study of international politics. Overcoming this problem is a question of mindset rather than a question of definition.

Another part of the reason so many scholars in the field talk past each other when discussing issues of paradigm and epistemology, however, is simple terminological confusion. Scholars tend to redefine terms frequently, creating a situation in which the same term is used by different authors with very different meanings. This observation holds for most of the key terms in this book, and certainly for the two main concepts: constructivism and realism. The confusion is exacerbated by individual authors who provide different definitions for the same words. For example, Alexander Wendt speaks of both political and scientific realism, arguing that the two are incompatible.[1] He also provides two definitions of idealism, as the -ism of ideas and the -ism of ideals – two quite different concepts. Discussions of idealism and scientific realism will appear in various places throughout the book, but these are not the core terms under discussion here. A first step in creating an effective conversation across paradigmatic lines, therefore, is to create clear working definitions of the two terms most

---

[1] Wendt 1999.

central to this book, realism (political) and constructivism, and to specify how they will be used here.

There are a number of different ways to go about the task of defining approaches to the study of IR. There is what might be called the expansive way, defining the approaches as broadly as possible. Thus, for example, if realists often focus on the state, any approach to the study of IR that focuses on the state must be realist. If constructivists speak of the importance of ideas, then any discussion of ideas in the context of international politics must be constructivist. The virtue of the expansive way of defining approaches is that it generates paths of exchange among scholars – if a given approach is defined broadly enough, then we all must be using it, and therefore we can communicate in its terms.

But the expansive way of defining approaches has its vices as well, chief among them that it waters down the analytic utility of the concepts underlying the approaches, and it has a tendency to intellectual imperialism. It waters down the analytic utility of concepts by including too much within them. If we define realism or constructivism broadly enough to include everyone, then to describe a piece of research or analysis as realist or constructivist tells us nothing useful about it. We then need to come up with other descriptors to distinguish among different concepts. But if we in turn define those descriptors too broadly, we need to create yet other descriptors, and so on in infinite regress. Expansive definitions in this sense are just not particularly useful in drawing distinctions among approaches.

Expansive definitions to approaches are also prone to intellectual imperialism. If an approach to the study of IR is defined broadly enough to include almost everyone, then the implication can be drawn that work that fails to fit within this expansive definition must be a real outlier, and thereby easily dismissed. Such definitions can therefore easily become tools of paradigmatic warfare, by co-opting personnel from other paradigms. A similar tactic can be seen in the opposite of expansive definitions, what might be called dismissive definitions. This way of defining a concept does so sufficiently narrowly that little or no work fits within the definition, meaning that work that does fit, or that claims to be using an approach even if it does not fit the dismissive definition, can similarly be easily dismissed. An example of this tactic can be found in Jeffrey Legro and Andrew Moravcsik's "Is Anybody Still a Realist?" They define as realist only those approaches that assume that states are rational unitary actors, that they have purely conflictual goals, and that only material capabilities are relevant.[2] They then go on to argue that by this definition, there are no realists. In fact, by this definition there never were any realists, because the definition is designed for rhetorical purposes to be a null set (all three elements of this definition are discussed, and dismissed, below).

A third way of defining approaches might be called the big-tent way, in which a definition is structured so as to include within it everyone who claims to be using the approach. Thus constructivism comes to refer to those calling themselves constructivists, and realism comes to refer to all those calling themselves realists. But in the end this use of terms is sociological rather than definitional – it is about building groups or scholars, rather than elaborating the concepts that they use. And building groups of scholars in this way can easily lead to paradigmatic castles, by creating groups that exchange ideas only among themselves.[3]

The definitions developed here begin by isolating core concepts within approaches to the study of international relations. This way of defining approaches shares superficial features with both big-tent definitions (because core concepts tend to be those invoked often by self-proclaimed practitioners of an approach) and expansive definitions (because core concepts are often the ones pointed to in these definitions). But it differs from the former in that in the end it focuses on the concept rather than the social group, and from the latter in that it develops coherent treatment of concepts rather than focusing on terms. As such, it is much less inclusive, as it applies only to work that focuses on those concepts, rather than all work in which reference to a general set of terms is made. For example, to the extent that realism is about power politics (and I shall argue below that it is), an expansive definition would count as realist any study of international politics that mentions power. But a core-concept definition would categorize as realist only such work as focuses on power politics, defined in a specific conceptual way.

These definitional questions will come up again, and will be discussed in more detail, in Chapters 8 and 9, the discussions of the

---

[2] Legro and Moravcsik 1999.
[3] But for an argument in favor of defining approaches in this way see Sterling-Folker 2009.

limits of realism and constructivism respectively. For the time being, the key upshot of this discussion of definitional styles is that the definitions that follow attempt to identify core concepts within each approach, rather than building more elaborate definitions or focusing on inclusiveness. This sort of definitional style will inevitably prove contentious, because arguments could inevitably be made in favor of other potential core concepts. But it is necessary for the task at hand, because mapping the relationships among approaches requires conceptual clarity, even if such clarity comes at the expense of inclusiveness. And this process of mapping is a necessary part of thinking about approaches as relating to each other, rather than as exclusive paradigms.

Before beginning with a definition of realism, however, a note on some of the other paradigmatic terms I use at various points in this book. I generally use these terms to refer to a core concept or core concepts, and I try to provide a clear indication of what those concepts are. For example, I use the term "critical theory" to mean an approach to the study of international relations that is "reflective upon the process of theorizing itself" and that "open[s] up the possibility of choosing a different valid perspective from which the problematic becomes one of creating an alternative world."[4] In other words, the core concepts of critical theory are the politics of theorizing, and the emancipatory potential of examining those politics. While there are certainly grounds for disagreeing with this specific choice of core concepts, it does provide a definition that is in keeping with most uses of the term in the discipline.

The other term to define at the outset is the one that shares a core disciplinary paradigmatic duopoly with realism, and that is "liberalism."[5] Writing a book about the relationship between realism and constructivism entails at least some discussion of liberalism, but a clear definition of the term is elusive. One could argue that the core concept underlying liberalism writ large is the assumption of the individual as the ontological starting point of political and economic discourse.[6] This ontological individualism can either be normative

---

[4] Cox 1986, pp. 207–208.
[5] The term "liberalism" is being used here in its political theory sense, not in the way it is used in colloquial American political discourse.
[6] For example Macpherson 1962.

(approaches that argue for the individual as a normative starting point) or epistemological (approaches that assume the individual as an empirical starting point). The identification of ontological individuality as the core concept of liberalism, however, still leaves quite a wide array of specific approaches covered.

There is one specific subset of liberalism that is particularly relevant to the various arguments in this book, both because it is a variant most commonly found in disciplinary international relations, and because it provides the rhetorical foil to realism. This is the variant that E. H. Carr referred to as liberal utopianism, and that Hans Morgenthau referred to as scientific liberalism.[7] The core concept of this variant of liberalism is the idea that if social institutions can be perfected, they can obviate power politics.[8] The form of this variant most commonly found in the contemporary study of international relations is neoliberal institutionalism, which is premised on the argument that the right set of institutional incentives will necessarily improve international cooperation.[9] The link between liberalism and perfectibility is discussed in more detail in various places below, but it seemed worth noting at the outset that this concept of perfectibility, as well as the broader concept of ontological individualism, informs the usage of the term liberalism here. This observation brings us back to the definition of the two key terms of this book, realism and constructivism.

Realism

Different schools of realism abound. Mirroring this diversity, definitions of realism abound, some that seem, on their face, to be mutually incompatible. To get to the point, I focus on classical realism, and argue that the core concept of realism is power politics, and that most other definitions of realism are descendent of power politics. The claim that power politics is the core concept of realism may seem to some readers obvious to the point of banality. But many contemporary definitions of realism give power politics little prominence and fail to indicate the extent to which they ultimately rely on it.[10] To

---

[7] Morgenthau 1946; Carr 1964.
[8] See, for example, the discussion of consensus in Geuss 2002.
[9] See, for example, Keohane 1984; Martin and Simmons 1998.
[10] For example Mearsheimer 1994/1995; Jervis 1998; Legro and Moravcsik 1999.

other interpreters of realism, power politics understood as *realpolitik* seems too prone to a narrow interpretation as the politics of brute force.[11] Some critics of realism associate it with broader concepts of power more generally, and argue that this is too broad a category to be particularly useful in the analysis of international relations.[12]

I am using the term "power politics" here in a specific way, as a much more circumscribed concept than that of power more generally. The broader concept of power is a highly contested one in the field of international relations,[13] and I make no claims here that the concept of power politics as I use it is more important for understanding international relations than other concepts of power. But I do make the claim that the concept is core to classical realism. Realist power politics is relative, relational, and social (note that my use of these three terms, as defined below, does not necessarily reflect a standard usage in IR theory – I distinguish among them to make specific points in this particular context). All three of these specifications of the realist use of the concept of power politics will prove important to the arguments being made in this book.

Realist power politics is relative, rather than being absolute, meaning that the power that can be brought to bear by an actor in this context is meaningful relative to the power of another state (or other social entity). It makes no sense to speak of the power of a state without the context of the object with respect to which or whom that power may be used. This definition is in direct contrast to the way in which power is conceptualized by physicists. In physics, a Watt is a standard measure of a unit of power, defined as one kilogram per meter squared per second cubed, regardless of the object upon which that power is used. There is, in other words, an absolute and objective measure of power. There is no equivalent measure in realism to a Watt. Even raw military power is contingent both on the motivation, as well as the hardware, of the adversary, and on the political context that defines what constitutes an effective use of power.

But, one might respond, given enough hardware a state can always simply destroy an adversary. This brings us to the second specific delimitation of realist power politics, that it is relational. The objects

---

[11] Williams 2005.   [12] See, for example, Wendt 1999, pp. 96–97.
[13] Compare, for example, Baldwin 1979, Guzzini 1993, and Barnett and Duvall 2005.

of power in this context are agents, not the passive objects of physical power. In politics, power is about getting other actors to do what you want them to do, which you cannot do if you have just destroyed them. Sometimes destroying them is, for broader geopolitical reasons, not a viable option. For example, military power gives the United States the ability to kill most of the inhabitants of any given country should they so choose. But, for a variety of reasons, the United States does not consider doing so to be in its national interest. That same military power, however, does not seem to give the United States the ability to install its chosen form of government in many of those same countries, even though this has often been defined as part of its national interest. In any context in which ends cannot reasonably be achieved by physically destroying an adversary, then, political power is ultimately about persuasion, about convincing rather than forcing.[14] And an ability to convince an actor to do what you want it to do depends on the interests of that actor as well as one's own power.

An exception to the observation that realists see power as relational can be found in John Mearsheimer's *The Tragedy of Great Power Politics*.[15] He argues that if one defines power relationally, then the only way to measure it is to look at outcomes, and then it becomes impossible to calculate the balance of power *ex ante*. But this implies that we have no ability whatsoever to judge the effects of political actions on their intended audiences. If this is the case, then we have no basis for making decisions about what political actions might work in changing the behavior of other actors in international relations. In other words, if this is the case then realism ceases to be the basis for making foreign policy prescriptions. Mearsheimer's argument is intended to privilege material over non-material measures of power, but he never successfully makes the case that material and non-material measures are relationally distinct. In other words, his argument is circular: he assumes that only material capabilities can be measured, and concludes that therefore only material capabilities can be measured.

This relational aspect of power politics distinguishes it from power as the term is often understood by critical and postmodern theorists of international relations. Michael Barnett and Raymond Duvall,

---

[14] On power as relational, see Dahl 1961; Baldwin 1979.
[15] Mearsheimer 2001, pp. 57–60.

for example, distinguish between interactive power, which involves influence wielded by certain actors over others, and structural power, which they define as "structural positions – that define what kinds of social beings actors are."[16] They argue that realism has biased understandings of power in the discipline of international relations too far toward the interactive, and that more attention should be given to structural power. This point is well taken on its own merits, but it does serve to highlight the relational understanding of power politics in realism. I use the term "power politics" rather than simply "power" specifically to underscore this relational focus ("power politics" implying a power that is self-consciously used, rather than structurally diffuse).

Finally, power politics for realists is social, or in other words corporate. Realists speak of the power of the state as a corporate actor, rather than the power of individuals. In other words, realists ascribe relational power, and therefore interests and agency, to social institutions, rather than to individuals. This tends to be done by assumption, rather than by argument.[17] Despite the absence of a well-developed realist ontology of the sociality of power, however, there is an ontology implicit in this understanding of power, which will be developed at some length in Chapter 4. This definition of power politics as social is distinct from the concept of power as structural in much the same way as is the case with power as relational. For realists, power is something that is used, rather than something that exists in a social hierarchy even absent intentionality. This distinction is discussed in greater detail in Chapter 5.

One way to make the case for power politics as the core concept of realism is to look at the range of definitions of realism that exist, noting the extent to which they are ultimately derived (both historically and logically) from propositions about the centrality of power in international relations. These propositions themselves can be found in seminal works of classical realism. The term "realism" came into the IR discourse in reference to the need to study international politics as they are, not as we feel they should be.[18] The logic behind this need

---

[16] Barnett and Duvall 2005, pp. 52–53.
[17] But see Carr 1964, pp. 157–162; Lobell, Ripsman, and Taliaferro 2009.
[18] See Schuman 1933; Rommen 1944; Kirk 1947; Morgenthau 1948; Carr 1964.

centered around power politics. We cannot, by wishing politics were different, make them so because we do not have the power; therefore, we must work within the existing balance of power.[19] One of the first and most influential major works developing realist international relations theory in the United States explicitly defined realism as being about power politics. Hans Morgenthau made all the study of international politics about power by definitional fiat.[20] He defined politics as the social science concerned with power, understood relationally. If we were to study some element of international relations that did not revolve around power politics, we would be studying international economics, or international law, or international sociology rather than international politics. In taking this stance, Morgenthau was not arguing that international law, economics, or sociology are irrelevant. What he was saying, however, is that, in the international domain, politics defined as power is important and merits study in its own right.[21]

In the more than half a century since Morgenthau's *Politics Among Nations* was first published, in 1948, this basic definition of realism has been built upon to the point that power politics, the original kernel of the definition, has occasionally gotten lost. Beyond power politics, contemporary definitions of realism usually contain some combination of the following: the analytic centrality of states, their interest in survival, the primacy of material capabilities, and rationality.[22] Together these elements show a clear lineage from the core classical realist concept of power politics, but often with little recognition of how they relate to the ideas from which they descend. Looking at these concepts one at a time allows us to reconnect them.

Many contemporary definitions of realism assume that the state is the central actor in international politics. For early realists, this premise was more a matter of observation than of assumption or deduction. The major political events during the first half of the twentieth century were the two world wars, and these wars were fought by and between states. States were the organizations in international politics able to organize and deploy power effectively. Indeed, no other organizations could deploy much effective power

[19] Lasswell 1935; Wight 1946; Morgenthau 1948; Carr 1964.
[20] Morgenthau 1985, pp. 31–32.   [21] Morgenthau 1948, p. 15.
[22] For a review of definitions of realism, see Donnelly 2000.

internationally; therefore states mattered. Consider, for example, E. H. Carr's conclusion that although states were currently the locus of power in global politics, they need not necessarily remain the central actor. "Few things are permanent in history; and it would be rash to assume that the territorial unit of power is one of them."[23] Since then states have, almost by habit among realists, been presented as a definitional element of realism in their own right.[24] One effect of this removal of states from observational to definitional centrality is the argument, advanced by both critics of realism and some neorealists, that what happens within states does not matter to realists. But few realist theorists (and few early neorealist theorists, for that matter) make this argument. In realist theory, what goes on within the state both determines the extent to which states are powerful and defines what their goals for that power are.[25] Classical realist theory is, in fact, very much a first image theory, which was Kenneth Waltz's critique of it, and the point of departure for his argument for neorealism.[26] Attempts by IR theorists, such as Legro and Moravcsik,[27] to draw the distinction between realist and liberal theory by proposing that the former is necessarily a third-image theory and the latter combines both first- and second-image theories are, thus, historically tenuous. In the evolution of realist logic, states matter in international relations to the extent that they have power; people and domestic institutions matter because they determine how much power states will have, and how it will be used.

The assumption that states share an interest in survival flows from the premise of state centrality. For some realists, assuming an interest in survival is a generalization rather than a categorical rule: states that are not interested in their own survival are not likely to last in an anarchical world. Therefore, we can assume that those states that have lasted and populate our contemporary world are those with an

---

[23] Carr 1964, p. 229.
[24] See, for example, Jervis 1998. Mearsheimer 2005, in making the case that power politics are central to realism, assumes without discussion that it is states that hold power.
[25] Note that Kenneth Waltz 1979, pp. 121–122, refers to this sort of thing as the study of foreign policy as distinct from the systemic study of international politics and argues that it can only be done in a reductionist way. But he never dismisses it as unimportant.
[26] Waltz 1959; Waltz 1979.   [27] Legro and Moravcsik 1999.

interest in survival.[28] Survival need not be the only, or even the key, motivator of state behavior; in situations in which power is relevant, however, states are likely to take it into account. Some critics of realism contend that the assumption that states value survival borders on the trivial, and there must therefore be some further implicit assumptions in realism about state preferences.[29] But the triviality of this assumption is precisely the point. In a world in which power matters, states need only have in common a basic concern for survival to think in terms of relative power.[30] Nor is the assumption of an interest in survival accepted across all schools of contemporary realism. Offensive realists, for example, argue that states are motivated by power maximization rather than survival, an assumption that projects classical realist arguments about human nature onto an anthropomorphized and power-seeking state.[31]

The third concept that often appears in contemporary definitions of realism is rationality. To many, perhaps most, current students of political science, the term "rationality" invokes rational choice theory.[32] This approach to the study of politics begins with the premise that we can usefully assume political actors, given their exogenously defined preferences, are instrumentally rational. The use of rationality in the context of realist theory, however, does not originate with the assumptions of rational choice theory. Two elements to the discussion of rationality arise in classical realism. The first is that we, as scholars, should be rational, which is to say ordered and "scientific" in a loose usage of that term, in our study of politics. In other words, we should look for general patterns of behavior, an admonition accepted by a wide range of (though certainly not all) social scientists.[33] The second way in which rationality

---

[28] Morgenthau 1948, p. 13; Waltz 1979, pp. 74–77; Jervis 1998, pp. 980–981.

[29] See, for example, Legro and Moravcsik 1999, p. 14; Wendt 1999, p. 235.

[30] See, for example, Waltz 1979; Grieco 1997; Schweller 1998.

[31] Rose 1998; Mearsheimer 2001.

[32] Kahler 1998; Katzenstein, Keohane, and Krasner 1998.

[33] This admonition, however, does not imply a commitment to a pure deductive model of social science, the model ascribed to rationalists by constructivists such as John Ruggie (1998, p. 880) and Alexander Wendt (1999, p. 48). Morgenthau 1946, in fact, used the term "scientific man" – one who would deduce solutions to the problems of international politics from first principles – as his polemical foil to realists in the same way that Carr 1964 used "utopians."

is discussed in realism is prescriptive rather than predictive – not that statespeople necessarily will behave rationally, but that in order to effectively pursue the interests of their states they should. That is, if national policy-makers want to make a difference rather than just a statement in international politics, they must rationally marshal their power resources. In Morgenthau's words, "foreign policy ought to be rational in view of its own moral and practical purposes."[34] Thus, what is often read as an assumption of rationality is, in point of fact, a prescription for rationality based on an assumption of the central-ity of power politics. The concept of rationality in the context of a realism/constructivism conversation will be discussed in more detail in Chapter 4, while the prediction/prescription distinction will come up again in Chapter 8.

The fourth concept, the assumption of the primacy of material capabilities, is something more often ascribed to realist theory by its critics than claimed by realists themselves.[35] Realists, it is true, often focus more on military power than on other sources of power, be they economic, organizational, or moral.[36] This predisposition can be attributed to the assumption that the military power of an adversary can threaten the very existence of a state, whereas other forms of power cannot. (Whether or not this assumption is accurate is open to debate.) This focus can also be ascribed to the context in which much of the seminal realist work took place, the Cold War,[37] or to the ease with which the tools of military power can be counted. But in situations in which no imminent military threat exists, as is currently the case among many of the world's major powers, no a priori rea-son exists within realist theory to privilege military power over other sources of power. During the Cold War, there was a cottage industry in counting up military manpower and hardware that owed more to the behavioral revolution than to realist theory, and it is, perhaps, from this development that realism has come to be associated with material capabilities.[38] But few realist theorists subscribe to such an

---

[34] Morgenthau 1985, p. 10.
[35] See, for example, Kratochwil 1984, p. 310; Wendt 1999, p. 30.
[36] For example, Mearsheimer 1994/1995.   [37] See Oren 2000.
[38] It is important to note, however, that the most dedicated of the counters of material capabilities, such as those involved in the Correlates of War project, described themselves as peace theorists or conflict resolution theorists and as anti-realist (see, for example, Singer 1990; Vasquez 1998).

assumption,[39] and many argue explicitly that the sources of power are non-material.[40]

When the assumption of materialism is largely ascribed to realism by its critics, then, one has to wonder why this particular straw man is being created. One reason might be to make realism more compatible with rational choice theory. It can, in fact, allow us to treat power the way that formal theorists treat preferences.[41] For classical realist theory, however, power is at least partially endogenous: one cannot know how much power one has without knowing how it is being used. The materialization of power resources has the effect of making power an exogenous variable; it becomes something that is out there, measurable and independent from immediate political activity. Formal theory must similarly take the preferences of actors as exogenous to the game being played. So through the materialization of power, realism becomes "rationalized" both for rationalists and their critics.[42] The topic of materialism is the focus of Chapter 3.

The discussion to this point implies that power politics is the core, and common, element of realist theory. Of the four concepts imbedded in contemporary definitions of realism, the analytic centrality of states and an interest in survival are descended from the original realist focus on power politics; the third concept, rationality, when used in the classical realist rather than the rational choice manner, suggests a focus on power politics as well. The fourth, the primacy of material capabilities, is more an effect of the behavioral turn in political science research during the mid-Cold War period and its rationalist turn in the late-Cold War period than an expression of a core realist idea.[43] And, yet, it is this fourth feature, rather than a focus on power politics, that is most often invoked to argue that realism and constructivism are incompatible.

---

[39] A notable exception here is Mearsheimer 2001, whose discussion of power is in any case problematic in its argument against understanding the concept as relational.

[40] See Waltz 1979, p. 131; Morgenthau 1985, pp. 34–36.

[41] Williams 2005, pp. 145–152.

[42] For example, Legro and Moravcsik 1999 and Wendt 1999 respectively.

[43] On the effects of the behavioral revolution on the mainstream of realist theory, see Guzzini 1998.

Constructivism

As with realism, definitions of constructivism abound, many of which are largely orthogonal to each other. These speak variously of ideas, norms, constitutive rules, and the social construction of identity and interests. They divide constructivism into categories, such as "thick" and "thin" or "postmodern" and "neoclassical."[44] The punchline of this discussion is that the core concept that connects all of these definitions is a focus on the social construction of international politics.[45] Social construction means that "social relations *make* or *construct* people – *ourselves* – into the kinds of beings that we are. Conversely, we *make* the world what it is, by doing what we do with each other and saying what we say to each other."[46]

As with the argument that power politics can be seen as the key concept of realism, defining constructivism in international relations theory as being about the social construction of international relations might seem at first obvious to the point of banality (after all, it is mostly a simple repetition of the name of the approach). But implicit in this focus are some significant methodological and ontological considerations. Among these considerations are two key components to the concept of social construction: intersubjectivity and co-constitution. Intersubjectivity in this context has been defined as "collective knowledge and understandings,"[47] "knowledge [that] persists beyond the lives of individual social actors, embedded in social routines and practices as they are reproduced by interpreters who participate in their production and workings."[48]

A useful way of clarifying what intersubjectivity means is discussion of what it does not mean. Specifically, it is a focus on neither the objective nor the subjective. That it is not objective implies a focus on ideas and understandings, rather than objectively given (or objectively deducible) conditions. We could presumably intersubjectively recognize a set of objectively given conditions, but then it would make more sense for analysis of international politics to focus on the objective conditions that are ultimately driving outcomes, and skip the dense

---

[44] These two dichotomies come from Wendt 1999 and Ruggie 1998 respectively.
[45] For example Klotz and Lynch 2007.
[46] Onuf 1998, p. 59 (emphasis in the original).
[47] Sterling-Folker 2006b, p. 116.   [48] Adler 1997, p. 321.

social theory. Implicit in the concept of intersubjectivity is the notion that it is the fact that we hold ideas and understandings in common, rather than any objective status of those ideas and understandings, that matters in international relations. Ideas and understandings in this context can refer to a number of things, including norms, identities, and discursive patterns. They may be explicit (recognized as such by those who hold them) or implicit (constitutive of discursive patterns or normative structures, but not self-consciously recognized by some or all of those who are part of the intersubjectivity). The intersubjective/objective distinction is often confused with an ideal/material distinction, and in this context is discussed in Chapter 3.

A focus on the intersubjective rather than on the objectively given as the motive source of international politics should not be confused with a rejection of the objective as a matter of research methodology. This observation gets us back to the thick/thin, or postmodern/neoclassical, distinction noted above.[49] Thick, or postmodern, constructivism does in fact accept the premise that we cannot objectively study intersubjectivity. Postmodern constructivists argue that attempts by scholars to find intersubjective norms will likely yield the ideas projected by the researcher onto the subject of study, rather than the ideas held in common by those subjects. As such, postmodern constructivist research tends to focus on the discursive construction of intersubjectivity (discourse being something that we can observe), rather than norms (which must be imputed from other evidence).

Thin, or neoclassical, constructivists, on the other hand, argue that there is a social reality out there that we can come to understand through observation of patterns of social interaction. A common way of doing this is through appeal to scientific realism[50] (a completely different and unrelated concept to political realism), the proposition that the world exists independently of our observations of it, and that scientific theory refers to this world, even when we cannot directly observe parts of this objective reality. In the context of constructivism, a scientific realist stance assumes that "[t]he state and states

---

[49] But see Klotz and Lynch 2007 for the argument that the distinction is not in fact that distinct, and is not that important at the level of research methodology.

[50] Patomäki and Wight 2000 refer to philosophical realism rather than scientific realism, but for the purposes of the argument here the two terms can be used interchangeably.

system are real structures whose nature can be approximated through science."[51] For this approach to constructivism, then, international relations is intersubjectively constructed rather than objectively given, in that the social structure of international politics does not exist prior to or outside of the mutable norms and discourses that define the identities and interests of actors. But that social structure, and the ideas that it is constructed of, is itself an objective reality that we can discover, or at least approximate, empirically.

Implicit in the concept of intersubjectivity is also that it is distinct from subjectivity. People must hold ideas or discourses in common, rather than just hold them individually. Ideas or discourses in this sense do not construct social reality until held in common within society. That a particular statesperson, for example, reacts to a provocation from abroad by thinking by analogy with Chamberlain's visit to Munich in 1938 does not make the Munich analogy a social construct. If others do the same, however, and if a discourse drawing on the analogy resonates with a public at large, the idea of a Munich analogy becomes a social construct.[52] This distinguishes constructivism from "first image" approaches to the study of international relations[53] such as political psychology and political cognition, as well as from deconstructive approaches to textual analysis, which tend to focus on the subjectivity of text.

A second key component of the concept of social construction is co-constitution. "In simplest terms, people *and* society construct, or constitute, each other."[54] Understood as such, constructivism looks at neither the effects of existing norms and discursive patterns on individuals, nor the role of individuals in creating norms and discursive patterns, in isolation from each other, but at both together. In other words, constructivism gives neither agents nor structures ontological priority, but argues that in the study of politics the agents and structures need to be viewed as simultaneously constituting each other. There are differences of opinion as to how best to interpret the agent–structure dialectic, but some form of the concept of co-constitution is

[51] Wendt 1999, p. 47.
[52] On the role of historical analogy in foreign-policy decision-making, that discusses the Munich analogy, see Jervis 1976.
[53] The language of images in international relations as used here is drawn from Waltz 1959.
[54] Onuf 1989, p. 36.

necessary to allow both for the social construction of politics and for change in that construction.[55]

Choosing the concept of social construction as the core concept defines constructivism in its own terms. But many definitions of constructivism try to define it in opposition to other approaches to the study of international relations. Two particular oppositions are found most commonly. One contrasts materialism with constructivist idealism.[56] The other draws on March and Olsen's distinction between the logic of consequences, when actors behave strategically to achieve objectives, and the logic of appropriateness, when actors behave according to identity scripts, doing what they believe to be expected of them in a given circumstance.[57] This opposition contrasts rationalism as a logic of consequences with norm-guided behavior based on a logic of appropriateness.[58] Both of these oppositions share neorealism as a common target from which to distance themselves, although the materialism opposition generally points to neorealism as an example of realism more generally, whereas the rationalism opposition is targeted more against "neo-utilitarianism," the group of approaches to international relations including neorealism and neoliberal institutionalism, that build from microeconomic theory.

At first glance, both of these oppositions, while they are not sufficient by themselves to define constructivism, might provide useful heuristics in distinguishing constructivism from other approaches to the study of international relations. But both oppositions prove to be problematic, and quite possibly more misleading than illuminating. Each is problematic on its own, for reasons that are discussed in the next two chapters. Taken together, they are problematic as defining characteristics of constructivism because they do not necessarily co-vary. One could, for example, rationally pursue an ideal, socially constructed goal. Or one could follow a logic of appropriateness socially constructed to reflect the material interests of another class.

Given that they need not co-vary, one can interpret the interaction of the two oppositions in two ways, as "both" or "either." In

---

[55] On the agent–structure dialectic, see Dessler 1989. On differing interpretations of co-constitution, see Pettman 2000, pp. 12–21.

[56] For example, Wendt 1999; Hopf 2002.

[57] See March and Olsen 1998, pp. 949–954.

[58] For example, Katzenstein, Keohane, and Krasner 1998; Ruggie 1998; Finnemore 1996b.

other words, if one were to accept both oppositions as definitional to constructivism, one could have constructivism defined as an approach to the study of international relations that applies only when actors act *both* according to a logic of appropriateness and in pursuit of ideal goals (or motivated only by non-material considerations). Or one could have it defined as an approach to the study of international relations that applies whenever actors act *either* according to a logic that is not purely strategic, or are motivated by considerations that are not purely material. The latter interpretation yields an operating definition of constructivism that is sufficiently broad that it yields little methodological or epistemological guidance. By this interpretation, for example, to the extent that money is a social construct, most of the science of economics as currently practiced accepts the ontology of social construction. This interpretation, in other words, runs into all of the problems of expansive definitions, taken to extremes. The former interpretation, on the other hand, is probably too narrow, and runs into problems of its own. In particular, a definition that focuses both on ideas as social structure and on a logic of appropriateness leaves too little room for agency in changing social structure. In other words such a definition would interact problematically with constructivism's focus on co-constitution.[59]

Both of these oppositions can be misleading in the impression they give about the relationship among various approaches to the study of international relations, by suggesting a greater space than is the case between constructivism and realism, and smaller spaces than are the case between these two and other approaches. As such, they provide a useful starting point for delineating a space for a realist/constructivist nexus in the study of international relations. The opposition between idealism and materialism is the topic of Chapter 3. A discussion of the opposition between the logics of consequences and appropriateness begins in Chapter 4.

---

[59] The logic of this claim will be explained further in later chapters.

3 | *Materialism*

An opposition of idealism and materialism is one of the two oppositions often used in definitions of constructivism, particularly in the United States.[1] But this simple dichotomization of these two concepts is misleading, in a variety of ways. It grossly simplifies what is in fact a more complicated relationship between the two concepts, in the process both creating a straw man of realism and confusing core definitional issues of constructivism. It confuses issues of ontology (the materiality of things) with issues of epistemology (whether or not we can study politics in the abstract). And it obscures relationships between both constructivism and realism on the one hand and various other approaches to the study of international relations on the other.

Idealism is itself a tricky term. Wendt distinguishes between idealism (the -ism of ideas) as a social theory of politics and Idealism (the -ism of ideals, which he capitalizes) as a theory of IR.[2] The first idealism refers to social theory that looks at the importance of ideas, whereas the second refers to a theory of IR based on ideals rather than on realism. It is in the former manner, as the -ism of ideas, that idealism is used by Wendt and others as a definitional component of constructivism, and it is with this definition that the term is used in this chapter. The other usage, idealism as the -ism of ideals, is discussed in Chapters 5 and 8. The materialist/idealist opposition as defined here refers therefore to the question of whether human behavior, and by extension the behavior of corporate social institutions, is ultimately motivated by brute material conditions or by ideas and discourses that constitute identities and interests.

[1] This is, for example, a distinction that forms a core of Wendt's construction of constructivism (Wendt 1999). Adler 1997 accepts the same distinction, but puts constructivism between materialism and idealism, rather than squarely on the idealist side.
[2] Wendt 1999, p. 33.

Using this opposition as a way to distinguish constructivism from realism makes strategic sense to the extent that realism has been the dominant approach to the study of international relations (although whether this dominance remains two decades after the first appearance of constructivism is certainly open to debate). Beyond realism, using this opposition can provide an effective rhetorical tool in establishing constructivism as a distinct approach. But, as Nicholas Onuf points out in the seminal work of constructivist theory, "the material and the social contaminate each other, but variably ... To say that people and societies construct each other is not to imply that this is done wholly out of mind."[3] There is no clear dividing line between ideas and physical material in social science, and to speak of the two in opposition has the effect of creating a false dichotomy. It also has the effect of distracting us from other related distinctions, such as that between subjectivity and intersubjectivity, and between transhistoricism and contextuality. The former is an ontological question, the latter two epistemological questions.

In turn, the use of an ideal/material opposition in the context of distinguishing constructivism from realism also has the effect of obscuring the relationship between both constructivism and realism on the one hand, and other approaches to the study of international relations that might be thought of as materialist, ranging from liberalism to Marxism to political psychology, on the other. Part of the task of this chapter, then, is to look at these relationships in the context of materiality in a way that goes beyond simple opposition.

Materialism and realism

The accusation of materialism by some constructivists against realism has two variants: the charge that realism focuses on material capabilities as a source of power, and the charge that realism requires certain assumptions about human nature, implying that human nature is determined by material biological factors. Not all constructivists, to be fair, subscribe to this accusation. But enough do that debunking it becomes pedagogically useful. That these charges create false dichotomies is discussed in the next section. But even given an opposition between materialism and idealism, both charges are inaccurate.

[3] Onuf 1989, p. 40.

The biological materialist charge is that realist logic requires certain assumptions about human nature and human needs that govern the behavior of actors in international politics.[4] The particular assumptions ascribed to realist understandings of human nature often include the presence of insecurity and fear.[5] It is true that realists must begin with some theory of human nature. As Wendt has observed, all social theory must begin with some theory of human nature, even if it is merely that human nature is infinitely malleable.[6] Moreover, there exist theories of human nature that are incompatible with political realism, including those that argue that human nature is infinitely malleable or ultimately perfectible. These are incompatible with realism because if human nature can be perfected or can be fully molded by the right social institutions, then a world can be created in which political power is no longer central to the management of human affairs. Realist logic therefore requires that human nature be to some extent at least imperfectible.

Beyond this general observation, however, realist logic does not require a specific theory of human nature. It does not require that all individuals be aggressive or self-interested, simply that some of them are. In other words, realism requires only that all individuals cannot be exclusively non-aggressive and other-oriented.[7] As long as some people will try to accumulate power, and no countervailing power stops them, other people face insecurity. This logic is, for example, the heart of Randall Schweller's distinction between status quo and revisionist states.[8] A more detailed discussion of biology and materialism comes in Chapter 7, in the context of a discussion of agency. A conclusion of that discussion is that there is a broad range of theories of human nature that are compatible with both realism and constructivism, suggesting in turn that the relationship among materialism, idealism, realism, and constructivism is more complicated than can be captured by simple oppositions.[9]

The charge that the realist understanding of power politics favors a focus on material capabilities was noted in the definitional discussion

---

[4] Wendt 1999, pp. 30 and 131–133.
[5] Waltz 1959; Wendt 1999. [6] Wendt 1999, p. 131.
[7] For a discussion of the variety of assumptions about human nature to be found in various realist theorists, see Freyberg-Inan 2004.
[8] Schweller 1998.
[9] For a general discussion of this literature, see Sterling-Folker 2002; see also Patomäki and Wight 2000.

of realism in the previous chapter. It is certainly the case that some self-described realist researchers have attempted to reduce the idea of power to quantitative measures.[10] But, beyond the fact that quantitative measures do not necessarily imply purely materialist measures, no reason exists to believe that such a procedure is inherent to realist theory. Indeed, the behavioralist turn in IR that brought with it a predilection for quantitative measures is generally considered to have happened decades after the realist turn, suggesting that the latter cannot be inherent to the former (this sequence of events is discussed at greater length in Chapter 8).[11] Many realist theorists, furthermore, have argued explicitly that non-material factors are central to a complete understanding of power politics in international relations.[12] Moreover, students of power analysis, some of them self-described realists, have pointed out how complex and multifaceted power analysis can be.[13] Even studies of military issues conducted by those calling themselves realists after the behavioralist turn often focused on such non-material elements as doctrine and threat.[14] The fact that some realist researchers use quantitative measures of brute material capabilities should, therefore, not be interpreted to mean that this sort of materialism is inherent in realism.

In fact, any claim that power politics can be reduced to measurements of material capabilities misunderstands the meaning of power politics in realist analysis. Power politics in this context is relative and relational. That it is relative means that actor A's power cannot be measured in its own terms, but only in comparison to actor B's.[15] If actor B chooses to respond to A's power in kind, then direct comparisons of capabilities are possible (although even then the capabilities may not be materially based). But if actor B chooses to respond to A's power with a different kind of power, then comparisons of material base, or of matériel, are beside the point. If A is using tanks and B is

---

[10] See, for example, Krasner 1976; Mearsheimer 2001.
[11] Vasquez 1983; Holsti 1985.
[12] See, for example, Morgenthau 1948; Wolfers 1962; Carr 1964; Waltz 1979; Gilpin 1981; Strange 1987; Walt 1987.
[13] See, for example, Lasswell and Kaplan 1950; Bachrach and Baratz 1962; Baldwin 1989; Hall 1997.
[14] See, for example, Mearsheimer 1983; Posen 1984; Walt 1987. Even Mearsheimer 2001, while claiming a purely material basis for power, argues that factors such as organizational skill need to be taken into account.
[15] For a discussion of power as a relative concept, see Baldwin 1979.

responding with guerrilla warfare, then statistics on number of tanks, or of economic potential, or any other material measure, are irrelevant. Measures of material capabilities can be relevant to specific political contexts, but those contexts are themselves contingent on ideas about what kind of power can and should be used, how it is to be used, and for what ends.

Realists generally recognize that power politics is contextual and relative, that material capabilities do not determine outcomes, and that outcomes are in any case contingent, as international politics are ongoing. This is why realists in the United States tended to oppose the decision to go to war with Iraq in 2003.[16] There was no doubt that the United States was overwhelmingly predominant in material capabilities at the time, and that these capabilities would yield a quick defeat of conventional Iraqi forces. But then what? Material capabilities could in this instance be instrumental in preventing one particular outcome, a continuation of Saddam Hussein's rule in Iraq, but predictably proved much less instrumental in generating the desired outcomes to replace it. The ultimate example of the limits of the material capabilities to destroy is thermonuclear weapons. They turn out to be of limited utility in the conduct of international politics in most instances specifically because materially they can do nothing other than destroy, and because of the social opprobrium associated with any potential use of them.[17]

Measures of pure material capabilities are even less useful when it comes to the relational aspect of political power than with the straightforward relative aspect. Political power is about getting others to do what you want them to do. A successful use of political power, therefore, depends as much on the cooperation of the actor(s) upon whom power is used as it does upon the goals and capabilities of the user. It depends upon what both the user and the target of political power understand both their own goals and the goals of the other to be. It is, in this sense, a form of persuasion rather than a form of brute force (and as such can be purely rhetorical).[18] At a highly aggregated level, this uncertainty about the effects of power on its

---

[16] See, for example, New York Times 2002.
[17] On which, see Tannenwald 1999.
[18] On rhetorical power in international politics, see *inter alia* Krebs and Jackson 2007 and Goddard 2009.

intended audience can be seen in the dispute in realist scholarship about the relative likelihood of balancing and bandwagoning behavior.[19] At a more specific level, to return to the Iraq example, whether Iraqis would greet US forces as liberators or occupiers in 2003 was a question that had great bearing on the success of the US use of force there, but was not something that could be determined from the material characteristics of that force.

Both the relative and the relational aspects of power politics are sources of the skepticism that realists tend to show about proactive foreign policies. E. H. Carr, for example, noted that traditional tools of foreign policy could not make foreign populations believe in the rightness of a policy, and on this perceptual rock even the best-intentioned foreign policies sometimes founder. "Power goes far to create the morality convenient to itself, and coercion is a fruitful source of consent. But when all these reserves have been made, it remains true that a new international order and a new international harmony can be built up only on the basis of an ascendancy which is generally accepted as tolerant and unoppressive."[20] Contemporary realists made the same argument about Iraq – force itself cannot make Iraqis into good democrats. To the extent that our goal is Iraqi democracy, therefore, material capabilities are not in themselves a determinative source of power. However much particular realists may engage in material resource-counting exercises, for realist theory those exercises do not meaningfully measure political power.

Materialism, idealism, and opposition

Are there then no materialists? Are we all then idealist? To a significant extent, these questions as asked are beside the point, because the two concepts are not in fact in direct opposition to each other. Politics, as is discussed in Chapter 7, requires agency, and agency in turn requires both ideas and materiality. Agency requires ideas because without thought as motivation, there is no agency, there is only inertia and reaction. And it requires materiality because ultimately one cannot dispense with assumptions about human material physiology. Theories of discourse require a material predisposition to

[19] See, for example, Schweller 1994; Rosecrance 2001.
[20] Carr 1964, p. 236.

communication skills. Theories that look to norms as a key element of political behavior assume a biologically based sociability that makes normatively based interaction possible. Trying to establish ontological priority for one or the other creates a chicken-and-egg problem (or, to use a more topical metaphor, an agent-and-structure problem); it is an infinitely recursive process that fails to yield useful insights.

Such an attempt to establish ontological priority also generates debates about whether a particular phenomenon is primarily material or ideal that are ultimately about definition rather than about substance. An example of such a debate can be found with the concept of money. Money is a social construct.[21] The point of money is that it has representational value, but no inherent use value. In other words, it has value only to the extent that we all collectively agree to accept its representation value in exchange for other things with use value. And yet, within its social construct, money tends very much to be an enabler of materiality. So much so that were a study to use national GDP (measured, of course, in money) as a proxy for international political power, it may well be accused of simple materialism. Is money then an ideal or material phenomenon? At a certain point, it simply does not matter.

One might respond that it does matter, because if money is a social construction, it is presumably historically contingent, as all social constructions are, but if it is a material phenomenon it may not be socially contingent. But to make this observation is to confuse ideas with historical contingency. A socially constructed international relations must be a historically contingent international relations, because if our intersubjective understandings of how politics can and should work change, the politics themselves will change. Two limitations of this observation must be noted, however. The first is that social constructs are not necessarily infinitely mutable. Actors can create social structures through practice, but this does not mean that they can create any social structure they want to. They may well have their own internal logics. Stated as a play on Alex Wendt's well-known aphorism,[22] anarchy may be what states make of it, but this does not necessarily mean that states can make of it whatever they want

---

[21] For discussions of the social construction of money, see, *inter alia*, Barkin 2003b and Helleiner 2003.
[22] Wendt 1992.

to. Social structures thus remain historically contingent, but given that they exist in a given time and place, they may be subject to fixed internal rules.[23] The second limitation is that not all approaches to the study of international relations that speak of social relations instead of or along with material conditions accept the idea of historical contingency. These two limitations are the subject of the next two sections of this chapter.

Taken together, these two observations suggest that the materialism/idealism opposition is easily confused with an opposition between historical contingency and transhistorical laws, and that this latter opposition is the more important to the process of defining constructivism. If a focus on materialism is incompatible with constructivism because it generates transhistorical givens that are incompatible with an understanding of politics as socially constructed, then the real problem is with the transhistorical givens, rather than with the materialism (this point should become clearer in the discussion of Kenneth Waltz and neorealism in the next section). Stated as such, the tension between contructivism and realism, despite any tendency on the part of the latter to fetishize military capabilities, is considerably less than that between constructivism and economistic approaches to the study of international relations, whether these approaches be from liberal or Marxist assumptions (I will come back to this argument in the section after next).

Materialism and transhistorical laws

The seminal use of the idealist/materialist opposition to distinguish constructivism from realism was by Alex Wendt in "Anarchy is What States Make of it." Wendt's specific target there is Waltz's version of neorealism, but Wendt extrapolates from that to all realisms. He argues that because Waltz does not accept shared ideas as structural elements of an anarchic state system alongside the distribution of capabilities, structure must be material rather than ideal.[24] The implication is that realists view capabilities as being purely materially based, even though few self-professed realists, including Waltz, do so. But there is also a logical flaw in the argument, which is the assumption that if a system is not intersubjective, it must be materialist. If

---

[23] Barkin 2003b.   [24] Wendt 1992.

a system such as anarchy is socially constructed, he argues, it must be the case that it can be constructed in a number of ways. The fact that Waltz argues for a single logic of anarchy therefore means that he must be using a materialist logic. But Wendt's argument on this point does not necessarily hold true. He discusses three logics of anarchy, implying that no single internal logic is inherent to anarchical systems. Ideal structures, however, can have their own necessary internal logics; those logics cease to affect the conduct of politics once the ideas themselves cease to be intersubjectively accepted. In other words, social constructs can generate specific internal logics, but those logics are not transhistorical laws, because the social constructs themselves can change.

An example of the difference between transhistorical laws and internal logics can be found in the realm of money. As noted above, money is a social construct. It only functions if we all accept the idea that we should be willing to trade things with actual use value for other things that have representational value but no inherent use value. This idea requires, among other things, huge amounts of trust that others will in future continue to recognize the representational value of the money, and will give us things of use value for it. It also requires that things of use value be available in exchange for money. It is certainly possible to have a complex society in which money is not the primary mechanism for allocating productive capital (this is the case, for example, both in barter economies and in centrally planned economies). So the use of money itself, as well as the details of particular monetary systems, is historically contingent.[25]

And yet, monetary systems have their own internal logic. One element of that logic is the relationship between the production of money and inflation. If the money supply grows faster than the supply of goods and services people want to buy, inflation results. This inflation happens whether the money is paper or metal, whether the increase in the money supply is the result of government decision (printing or debasing currency) or exogenous supply (for example, finding new sources of metal). One can have an economy without the social construct that is money. A society can choose not to increase the supply of money faster than demand, or it can decide that inflation is an acceptable side-effect of increasing the money supply (or

[25] Barkin 2003b.

even a desired effect). But it may well be the case that one cannot socially construct a political economy that uses money, in which the money supply can be expanded without inflationary effects, because of the internal logic of the system. This does not make inflation a transhistorical law, any more than it makes inflation a material thing. Inflation is an idea, one that is relevant only to particular, historically contingent social constructs. But it nevertheless inheres in the internal logic of those constructs.

Is the neorealist balance of power, in this sense, like inflation? It is, in the sense that it is a logic inherent to a structure that need not be materially based. The national capabilities that Waltz speaks of can be organizational or motivational rather than (or in addition to) material. In this sense, Waltz's neorealism is more compatible with constructivism than Wendt allows for. But the incompatibility that Wendt is trying to establish may have more to do with the issue of transhistorical laws than materialism *per se*. Nor is Wendt alone in confusing the issues of materiality and the historical fixity of system structure – in his critique of Wendt, Dale Copeland jumps from one to the other without distinguishing between them.[26] Focusing on the historically contingent/transhistoric distinction rather than on a material/ideal distinction allows us to study the social construction of systems with internal logics without worrying about a boundary between the material and the ideal that is fuzzy at best. It also allows constructivists to argue that systems effects that are sometimes taken for granted as givens may be given only within very specific, and therefore mutable, social constructions.

This still leaves the question of whether the neorealist balance of power is an internal logic or a transhistorical law. The answer to this question is confused by the fact that, as Wendt and others point out, Waltz is wrong in claiming that the units of the international system, states, do not share ideas in common. States are themselves social constructs, and the system that Waltz talks about exists as such only insofar as people within them think of them intersubjectively as the primary form of political organization.[27]

---

[26] Copeland 2000.
[27] For a discussion of Waltz's unitary conception of the state in comparative perspective, see Bartelson 1998. For a defense of looking at states as corporate actors nonetheless, see Wendt 1999, pp. 218–224.

The difference between a neorealist balance of power and inflation in this context, then, is intersubjectivity. Inflation is a logic internal to a historically contingent social system. It is only a relevant concept, in other words, to the extent that people accept coins, or little bits of paper, or electronic communications as money. If people do not participate in the use of an object of exchange as money, then it ceases to be money. To the extent that Waltz claims that states need not share ideas in common for his logic of anarchy to work, he is not talking about the logic internal to a social system. His logic of anarchy is not intersubjective. In his logic, states that fail to recognize that they are in an anarchical system are nonetheless subject to the effects of that system. This does not make the system materialist, but it does make it transhistorical, in the sense that it applies in all cases in the absence of a socially constructed hierarchy. He claims not that the logic applies in historically contingent situations, but that it applies in all cases except when there are certain specified historical contingencies (i.e. hierarchy, itself a social construction).[28]

The key incompatibility between constructivism and Waltz's version of neorealism, therefore, is not the idealism of the former versus the materialism of the latter. It is the intersubjectivity of the former, and its necessarily resultant historical contingency, versus the methodological individuality (or, as Wendt puts it, ontological unit reductionism[29]) of the latter, and its resultant transhistoricity. But this unit reductionism is largely particular to Waltz and neorealism (and even some other neorealists, such as Gilpin, explicitly note the importance of intersubjectivity to the states system[30]), and not to realism more broadly. Waltz does speak of states being socialized to the system, and therefore by implication of intersubjective norms.[31] But it is the system that is forcing the socialization, and therefore the norms can be expected to remain constant over time. As such, while there are intersubjective norms in Waltz's model, they are not being socially constructed.

---

[28] For a somewhat different take on Waltz's sociology, that nonetheless agrees with the claim here about his transhistoricity, see Goddard and Nexon 2005.

[29] Wendt 1987.   [30] Gilpin 1981.

[31] Waltz 1979, pp. 74–77.

Constructivism, liberalism, and Marxism

As with realism, there is some question as to whether or not both liberal and Marxist approaches to the study of international relations are inherently materialist. Liberalism is difficult to categorize in an idealist/materialist dichotomy because as a category it brings together so many strands of thinking. The more economistic strains of liberalism, such as utilitarianism, seem at first glance at least somewhat materialist. But even these strains are not ultimately materialist, because the content of individual utility is so unclear. Neoliberal economics often equates individual utility with market utility, which is measured in money, itself a social construct and usable to buy nonmaterial things. Social utilitarians such as John Stuart Mill argue that some forms of utility are better than others, but the better forms of utility seem to be the less material ones, such as that group of pursuits that might be labeled high culture.[32]

The case that Marxism is materialist seems at first to be much more straightforward. After all, Marxists often explicitly describe themselves as materialist (in the context of historical materialism). Three observations mitigate against so simple a conclusion, however. The first is the argument that Marxist materialism is about relations of production, rather than about production itself. The second is the psychological turn of much contemporary Marxism. And the third is the complex relationship between traditional Marxism and critical theory, which can make it difficult to determine what actually counts as Marxism (or as critical theory, for that matter). The extent to which one reads Marxist international relations theory as materialst, therefore, depends both on how one is choosing to define materialism, and to which strand of Marxist thought one is referring.

The argument that Marxist materialism is different from realist materialism because the former is about relations of production, whereas the latter is about physical things, is made most explicitly in the context of constructivist theorizing by Alex Wendt. He does this as a "rhetorical move ... which is justified by the fact that the traditional framing of the debate stacks the deck against idealism."[33] But Wendt's framing stacks the deck sufficiently against materialism as to make it a null set. Even military hardware, by Wendt's definition, is

---

[32] Mill 1863.   [33] Wendt 1999, p. 95.

ideal inasmuch as people have ideas about how to use it. Furthermore, political power for realists, as noted above, is relational in much the same way as the forces of production are relational for traditional Marxists. In short, it is difficult to imagine a definition of materialism that covers most of political realism that does not also cover many traditional Marxist and neo-Marxist approaches to the study of international relations.

Materialism in critical theory, which to an important degree developed from Marxist thought but which is generally far less economistic than Marx's own work (his later work in particular) and the work of Marxist IR theories such as world systems theory,[34] is less clear. In part this is because materialism *per se* is orthogonal to the core concepts of critical theory, and as such different strands of critical theory treat it differently. Some strands, including those descended from Frankfurt School theorizing and including such contemporary thinkers as Jürgen Habermas, marry social analysis with psychology, and therefore bring in some materialism through assumptions about the biology of the brain.[35] Other strands, most commonly associated in the international relations literature with Antonio Gramsci, retain Marx's focus on production and relations of production.[36] Both groups of strands can therefore be seen as materialist in some ways, but not necessarily in ways that make them incompatible with constructivism (given that we need to make some assumptions about the materiality of the brain, and that relations of production can well be studied as social constructions).

A focus on the opposition between materialism and ideas thus gets us no further in comparing constructivism with liberalism and Marxism than it gets us comparing constructivism with realism. The opposition is essentially false – there are ideas embedded in most socially meaningful physical material, and there is materiality embedded in the ability to create and communicate ideas. They are in a dialectical relationship, rather than in opposition. If, however, the rhetorical creation

[34] Wallerstein 1974 and 1979.
[35] Habermas' "will to reason," for example, implies an assumed tendency in people to prefer reason to other forms of interaction that can only be biological. See, for example, George and Campbell 1990, p. 279.
[36] For example, Cox 1987; Gill 1993. For a discussion of this approach to critical international relations theory in the context of international political economy, see Murphy and Nelson 2001.

of this opposition in the context of constructivism and neorealism is creating a distinction that is really about historical contingency and transhistoricity, then it may be the case that looking at this latter distinction will tell us more about the relationship among constructivism, liberalism, and Marxism than focusing on materialism.

Looking at transhistoricity does in fact tell us more about the relationship between constructivism on the one hand and liberalism and the more economistic variants of Marxism on the other than does looking at materialism. Both of the latter two approaches often tend toward transhistoricalism in ways that puts them in tension with constructivism in much the same way as Waltzian neorealism is in tension with constructivism. Economistic and utilitarian liberalisms are transhistorical in that they claim fixed patterns of human behavior in response to given institutional stimuli, irrespective of intersubjectively held ideas. In other words, if one designs political and economic institutions the right way, those institutions will elicit the predicted behavior. This practice can be clearly seen in neoliberal institutionalist approaches to the study of international relations, which argue that international cooperation depends on proper regime design.[37] It is also a core assumption of rational choice theory, which begins with the premise that all human thought, in all times and places, can usefully be described by a very particular kind of cost–benefit analysis (assuming either that people generally behave in such a manner, or, at the minimum, that rationality is an epistemologically or heuristically useful starting point). There are other liberalisms that are transhistorical in their normative rather than their empirical assumptions (which is orthogonal to the specific point being made here but which will come up again later in the book).

Traditional Marxisms that focus on class as a unit of analysis are similarly transhistorical, notwithstanding self-descriptions as historical materialism. They are transhistorical because they posit non-contingent stages of development, and because they posit "real" class interests in opposition to false consciousness.[38] To the extent

---

[37] See, for example, Keohane 1989; Mitchell 1994.
[38] There are, of course, huge literatures on such concepts as historical materialism and false consciousness, and the passing reference to these concepts here fails to do them, and scholars who study them, justice. But the basic point still holds.

that a key point of constructivism is that identities and interests are historically contingent, there is no "real" interest underlying the social construct, no intersubjectively constructed identity that is false. It is, as Wendt notes, ideas all the way down.[39] The intersubjective constructs are all there is, there is nothing behind them. The constructivist critique of neorealism as insufficiently historically contingent, then, can be applied equally to traditional Marxism, and by extension to approaches to international relations grounded in traditional Marxian economic and social theory. Marxism in this sense differs from neorealism in being ontologically reducible to the system rather than to the individual, but it is nonetheless reducible, rather than being grounded in the co-constitution of agent and structure.

The same argument about transhistoricity is true to varying degrees of various approaches to critical theory as well. Two popular touchstones for critical theory in the study of international relations are Antonio Gramsci and Jürgen Habermas. Gramscian approaches to international political economy (IPE), while they focus on the social relations of production, tend also to assume that these relations show some fixed patterns over time, even though particular social relations of production are historically contingent. Furthermore, they also allow that technology has a hand in determining these relations, that "the structure of authority [i]s molded by the internal dynamics of the production process."[40] Habermasian approaches, rather than looking to production as the key source of power, look to reasoned discourse as the key answer to power.[41] But in itself these approaches are also transhistorical, in that they claim that a certain structure of discourse can obviate the central role of power in social relations. This claim is general, not contingent. More recent Continental critical theory imports transhistoricity in various other ways. Slavoj Žižek, for example, drawing both on the Marxian tradition and on the work of Jacques Lacan, brings in transhistoricity through a Marxian theory of value. He offers as an example caffeine-free Diet Coke, and argues that because it has no intrinsic value as a beverage whatsoever, we need Lacanian psychoanalytic and discourse theory to understand why anyone would possibly want to drink it (he contrasts this with

[39] Wendt 1999.   [40] Cox 1987, p. 12.
[41] See, for example, Risse 2000.

beer, which does, he argues, have an intrinsic value).[42] Intrinsic value in this sense is both material and transhistorical, and it is the socially constructed value that needs to be explained away.

Historical contingency, epistemology, and ontology

Transhistoricity is the idea that we can study international politics in the abstract, whereas historical contingency is the idea that we can only study it in historical context. It is in this sense an epistemological stance. If it is transhistoricity rather than materialism that is the more fundamental issue in comparing the various approaches to the study of international relations discussed here, then what is presented by some constructivist scholars as an ontological issue (materialism/idealism) is really an epistemological one.[43] And recasting this opposition as an epistemological issue rather than an ontological one not only decreases the intellectual gulf between realism and constructivism. It also increases the intellectual tension between constructivism on the one hand and both most liberalisms and some Marxisms, including much critical theory, on the other.

Transhistoricity is therefore *a* key point of comparison among these approaches. But this should not be taken to mean that transhistoricity is *the* key point of comparison, or that epistemology is a more important axis of comparison than ontology.[44] Rather, it is a point of comparison, one dimension among many that do not necessarily co-vary. A good example of this sort of non-covariation can be found by comparing the epistemological issue of transhistoricity and historical contingency with the ontological issue of scientific realism.

As noted in Chapter 2, scientific realism is the idea that there is an objective reality out there, and that research allows us access to the contours of that reality, whether or not we can observe it directly. The idea of scientific realism is orthogonal to questions of materiality versus idealism and questions of transhistoricity versus historical contingency. The study of objective reality can be material and transhistorical, as would be the case with scientific realism applied to the

---

[42] Žižek 2000, pp. 21–23.   [43] Smith 2000 makes this point.
[44] There is a debate about whether ontology or epistemology is more important. See, for example, Wight 2006 and Smith 2000 respectively. I take neither side of this debate here.

study of physics or chemistry. But it can also be ideal and historically contingent, as would be the case as applied to the study of social systems.[45] For example, a scientific realist take on the categorization of chemical weapons in contemporary international politics as non-conventional would be that there is an intersubjectively understood rule that chemical weapons are normatively different from explosives. There is no necessary material or transhistorical reason for this categorization; it is a historically contingent norm, but from this perspective the norm is real and objective nonetheless.[46]

Scientific realism, given that it posits an objectively real world, is therefore ontologically more compatible with thin or neoclassical constructivism than with thick or postmodern constructivism.[47] These two constructivisms, then, are epistemologically compatible in their focus on historical contingency, but ontologically in tension in their disagreement over the existence of an objective reality. Similarly, classical Marxism and many contemporary approaches to critical theory are epistemologically compatible in their acceptance of transhistorical givens in the study of international relations, but ontologically incompatible in that classical Marxism is scientifically realist. Critical theory, on the other hand, to the extent that it is based on the premise that the theory through which we see the world makes the world that we see, is much less compatible with a scientific realist ontology.[48]

Neoclassical and postmodern constructivism thus have more in common with each other than with Marxism and critical theory with respect to the epistemological question of historicity. But on the ontological question of an objective reality, neoclassical constructivism and classical approaches to Marxism share more in common than either do with postmodern constructivism or critical theory, which in turn are ontologically compatible in this way. There are of course numerous other dimensions, both epistemological and ontological, on which these approaches to the study of international relations

---

[45] Wight 2006 makes the general case for a scientific realist approach to the study of IR.

[46] For example Legro 1995.

[47] For example, Doty 2000; Kratochwil 2000; Patomäki and Wight 2000; Wight 2007.

[48] A case can be made that critical theory is compatible with critical realism, a variant of scientific realism. But there is some dispute as to the relationship between the scientific and critical variants. See Kurki 2007 and Chernoff 2007 respectively.

might vary. The point here is that the relationships among various
approaches are non-linear and complex, and that focusing on an ideal/
material opposition confuses these relationships and their complexity
more than it illuminates them.

So what?

The core argument of this chapter is that using an idealism/material-
ism opposition as a definitional tool for constructivism is misleading,
in three key ways. All three of these figure prominently in the core
argument of this book, that there is a good argument to be made
that realism and constructivism have points of tangent, and that the
complexity of the relationships among constructivism, realism, and
the various other -isms of international relations theory should be cel-
ebrated rather than simplified. The idealism/materialism opposition
is misleading because it paints as an ontological distinction what is
really an epistemological distinction, because it creates a false tension
between realism and constructivism, and because it obscures questions of historicity that are central to both constructivism and to classical realism.

The ontology/epistemology distinction in this context is important
in developing an operational definition of constructivism because it
helps to position constructivism within an array of approaches to
the study of international relations, rather than positioning it simply
with respect to a straw man version of neorealism. The positioning
with respect to neorealism may well have been rhetorically effective
in carving out a space for constructivism within the social construct
of international relations as a profession in the early 1990s. But that
construct has changed over time, and in any case rhetorical utility is
not necessarily the best gauge of a definition.

Defining constructivism as ideal in opposition to realist materialism mischaracterizes most political realisms, and creates a false tension between the two. In particular, the opposition implies that realist
power politics, being somehow purely material, must be of a different species of thing than power as constructivists speak of it. While
constructivism can indeed draw on broader meanings of power than
does realist power politics, the latter is indeed compatible with constructivist understandings, being both relational and social. As such,
constructivism is well placed to answer what is a core question for any

realist policy analysis, the question of what constitutes power politics in a particular international system, with respect to a particular issue construction, at a particular point in time. It is well placed to look beyond easily counted proxies for power, to phenomena such as discursive power that fit squarely within a classical realist worldview. Creating false tension between these two approaches makes it more difficult to answer questions like these.

Finally, using the ideal/material opposition as a proxy for questions of historicity has the effect of both confusing the issue of historicity with the issue of materialism, and of confusing internal logics with claims of transhistoricity. Conflating materialism with transhistoricity is confusing because materialism in this context is really a red herring. Given the difficulty of separating the ideal from the material, whether something is defined as ultimately material depends on how one defines materialism. If one wants to define away the usefulness of "materialist explanations," define materialism narrowly. If one wants to explain politics as being materially based, define materialism broadly. It becomes a rhetorical game rather than an explanatory tool. Focusing on historicity helps avoid this rhetorical game, and focuses attention on the actual epistemological question at issue.

Confusing internal logics with transhistoricity is an important issue because presenting the idealism/materialism distinction as an opposition implies a dichotomous relationship – either a thing is material, and therefore fixed, exogenous to social construction, or it is ideal, socially constructed and therefore infinitely malleable. Materiality in this dichotomy is fixity, and to focus on materialism is to be unable to explain change. But idealism in this dichotomy has no fixity, and therefore to focus on it in this dichotomy is to be unable to explain continuity. To focus on transhistoricity rather than materiality as a foil for constructivist argument is to allow for internal logics within social constructs. And to allow for these logics allows constructivists to address both continuity and change. A similar problem of explaining both change and continuity also arises when using the other common opposition to define constructivism, that with rationalism.

4 | The logic of the social

The second of the oppositions often used in definitions of constructivism is that of rationalism with the logic of the social. The specific terminology of this opposition varies from author to author. For example, in the 50th anniversary issue of the journal *International Organization* that was organized around the opposition of rationalism and constructivism,[1] John Ruggie contrasts neo-utilitarianism with social construction.[2] Thomas Risse and Ted Hopf both contrast the logic of consequences associated with rationalism with the logic of appropriateness associated with constructivism.[3] Rationalists, in other words, see people making decisions using a strategic logic, based on what will maximize their individual interests. By this definition, by contrast, constructivists see people making decisions using a social logic, based on social norms and the expectations of others.

In one sense this is a perfectly reasonable opposition – an approach to the study of international relations that is based on the idea that politics are socially constructed must be based on a logic of the social. But putting rationalism as the concept in opposition to a logic of the social is problematic in two ways. The first is that it is not clear which concept of rationality is being opposed. In the end, what is being opposed is not the reasoned thought that classical realists referred to when speaking of rationality, but the methodological individualism of microeconomic theory. To the extent that Waltzian neorealism is grounded in microeconomic theory, conflating the two uses is effective as a critique. But most realisms are not grounded in this way, and the use of rationalism as the target of opposition then creates another false distinction between constructivism and realism.

---

[1] Katzenstein, Keohane, and Krasner 1998.   [2] Ruggie 1998.
[3] Risse 2000, p. 1; Hopf 2002, p. 12. Risse uses the phrase "logic of consequentialism," while Hopf uses "logic of consequentiality." Both use the phrase "logic of appropriateness."

The second way in which making rationalism the target of opposition to a logic of the social is problematic follows from a similar lack of clarity. In conflating methodology (rationalism as individualism) with psychology (rationality as the way in which people either do or should think) it confuses the question of what people think about with the question of how they think about it. Interesting questions both, but distinct. And the distinction is a critical one for constructivism, because the difference goes to the core of the logic of the social that underlies the constructivist approach. The critique of rationalism as individualism is a fundamental part of this logic. The critique of rationalism as psychology, however, at a certain point becomes incompatible with this logic.

What is a logic of the social? At its most basic, it is the idea that we cannot understand human society by aggregating from the behavior of individuals, whether this aggregation is inductive, as one finds with quantitative and opinion-based approaches to the study of international relations, or deductive, as one finds with rational choice approaches. Rather, we must start with the idea that human behavior cannot reasonably be studied apart from the social structures within which it occurs, and that give it meaning. Few if any constructivists would dispute this definition, stated as such. Nor is constructivism alone among approaches to the study of international relations in being grounded in a logic of the social, as is discussed below. As was the case in the discussion of historicity in the previous chapter, examining the relationships among these approaches on the axis of sociality yields interesting observations. One of the resulting implications is that constructivism shares its grounding in a logic of the social with classical realism. Another is that it does not share this grounding with many liberal, and some deconstructive, approaches.

Rationalism

Presenting the logic of the social as being in opposition to the logic of the rational seems at first glance to make sense. After all, rational choice theory is based on the idea that human behavior is driven by the rational pursuit of individual interests. Those interests are mediated through institutional structures that affect strategies and outcomes, but those structures do not affect actual individual interests, which are on this view ontologically prior to social institutions.[4] There is governance, but in the words of Margaret Thatcher, "there is no such thing as society."[5] This approach to social science is clearly incompatible with a logic of the social, in which the individual, and individual interests, cannot meaningfully be studied in isolation from social structure and social patterns of rules, norms, and discourses.

Michael Williams argues that the opposition, or polarity as he terms it, between rationalism and constructivism is false, because rationalism as understood in international relations theory is itself a social construction.[6] While his point is well taken as such, it concedes too much definitionally to rational choice theory. Stating the opposition in this way conflates rationality, the idea that people use reason as a decision-making or discursive tool, with rational choice theory, a very specific approach to the study of social science. Furthermore, it is not the appeal to reason in rational choice theory *per se* that is the primary site of its incompatibility with a logic of the social. It is the methodological individualism, the fact that rational choice theory is ontologically reducible to the individual, whereas a logic of the social is not. Social logics can be ontologically reducible to the social, as are some structural approaches to social science, but constructivism's ontological starting point is the interaction between the individual and the social.[7]

Invoking rationality need not invoke methodological individualism. In fact, invoking rationality in the study of international relations can mean a variety of different things. Rationality can be instrumental or communicative, meaning that it can be defined as the making of decisions based on analyses of costs, benefits, and efficiencies, or as an attempt to convince others in the public sphere through the use of reason.[8] It can be prescriptive (an exhortation for future behavior) or predictive (an assumption about all behavior). And it can be used in the context of the participant in decision-making, or the student of decision-making, or both.[9] Rational choice theory's use of the concept of rationality is instrumental, predictive, and focused on the

---

[4] Wendt 1987.
[5] For both a sourcing and a discussion of this quotation, see Oborne 2002.
[6] Williams 2005, pp. 145–159.   [7] Wendt 1987; Onuf 1989.
[8] For a discussion of communicative rationality, see Habermas 1984. For an application to international relations theory, see Risse 2000.
[9] See, for example, Elster 1983 and 1989.

participant in decision-making. All three of these aspects of the use of rationality are implicated in rational choice theory's methodological individualism. Classical realism's use of rationality shares none of these definitional features.

The invocation of rationality by classical realists was first and foremost prescriptive, not predictive. They exhort us to use reason to understand the world, rather than assuming that the world is a reasonable place. In fact, at times some of the seminal classical realists were specifically arguing against an approach to the study of international relations that assumes that the world is a rational place. In *Scientific Man Versus Power Politics*, for example, Hans Morgenthau argues that "scientific man," who would solve the problems of politics as a mechanical process, as social engineering, is incapable of successfully addressing those problems. "Scientific man" assumes that people will respond reasonably to incentives; the history of power politics suggests that this is not so.[10]

The same Morgenthau also argues, in *Politics Among Nations,* for "a rational theory ... that reflects the laws of politics."[11] This marks a second distinction from the concept of reason in rational choice theory, the distinction between reason on the part of the decision-maker and reason on the part of the student of politics. For Morgenthau, as for E. H. Carr,[12] a rational approach to the study of politics is one in which the student uses reason, rather than one in which it is assumed that the object of study uses reason. And using reason in this sense means that the student must actually think about politics as they are and as they have historically been, rather than mechanistically apply decision rules to political situations, as do rational choice theorists. Rationality here is used in the sense of reasonableness, rather than as a fixed set of rules about how people do or should think.

What has recently come to be called the English school of international relations is also sometimes referred to as the rationalist approach,[13] and it is this sense of rationality, as reasonableness, that is referred to in doing so. The English school of rationalists certainly has little in common with the rational choice theory approach to international relations.[14] It is interesting to observe in

---

[10] Morgenthau 1946.   [11] Morgenthau 1985, p. 5.
[12] Carr 1964.   [13] See, for example, Linklater 2001.
[14] See, for example, Copeland 2003.

this context that Christian Reus-Smit notes the similarities between constructivism and the English school approach in an essay in which he defines constructivism in opposition to rationalism, in a volume containing a chapter entitled "Rationalism" which uses the term to refer to the English school.[15] The term comes full circle within one volume.

The example of the English school as a self-described rational approach to the study of international relations is also interesting in this context because it is a rationalism that takes into account social expectations, that explicitly invokes international society.[16] It is in this sense a use of the term "rationalism" that is not compatible with methodological individualism, and one that has a long history in the discipline of international relations. It is in its focus on the importance of international society that, according to Reus-Smit, the English school is similar to constructivism.[17] This focus does seem to put English school rationalism somewhat at odds with classical realism's focus on power politics. But then classical realism often focused on using power politics specifically to maintain one's position in the international system without war. In this sense the distance between the two is not as far as it might at first seem, and in fact some scholars have argued that the English school is in ways a direct linear descendant of classical realism.[18]

The meaning of rationality as the term is used in classical realism, then, bears little conceptual relationship to the meaning as used in rational choice theory. Rationality in classical realism is neither predictive nor necessarily methodologically individualist. (That it has come in some recent rewritings of realism to be used as a predictor is discussed in Chapter 8, along with an explanation of how this change has undermined the prescriptive utility of classical realism.) Finally, rational theory for classical realism meant not that theory must be based on the rationality of those who are studied, but on the reasoning abilities of those who study, precisely the opposite of the way in which the term is used in rational choice theory.[19]

---

[15] Reus-Smit 2001a; Linklater 2001; Burchill *et al.* 2001.
[16] See, for example, Bull 1977.   [17] Reus-Smit 2001a.
[18] Dunne 1998.   [19] Barkin 2003a.

The logic of appropriateness

Positing rationalism as the opposite of the logic of the social therefore is confusing. Positing rational choice theory as methodologically incompatible with a logic of the social is reasonable, but for reasons of methodological individualism that do not apply to many uses of the term "rationality." Choosing rationalism as the term of opposition, therefore, distracts from the core issue. And it implies that constructivists assume, or argue, that people do not behave rationally, however rationality is understood. Some constructivists have compounded this misunderstanding by contrasting rational individualist behavior with more "social" behavior, in which people behave according to social norms rather than in pursuit of individual utility.[20] If the mode of behavior of the individual in rational choice theory can be thought of as following a strategic logic, the mode of behavior of the individual following social norms can be thought of as a logic of appropriateness.[21]

At the extreme, these two logics can be thought of as incompatible assumptions about human behavior. In fact, each of the logics, interpreted broadly, is tautological. Anything can be described as strategically rational behavior by imputing the utility structure of the individual in question that would make it so. For example, altruism is rational if an individual gains utility from the well-being of others, and suicide is rational if an individual's expected future utility is negative. In this sense, anything can be rewritten as a rational choice game, even the Bible.[22] Similarly, all behavior can be understood as responding to a logic of appropriateness, even behavior that is clearly goal-oriented, by identifying it as a social norm. If people are behaving that way, then it must be a norm, if one assumes that that is the way that people behave.

Being tautological, neither logic by itself is of much use in explaining any particular behavior, or in distinguishing any set of behaviors from any other. In this sense, defining constructivism in opposition to an assumption of rational behavior (rather than in opposition to

---

[20] See, for example, Risse 2000; Hopf 2002.
[21] The distinction between a logic of consequences and a logic of appropriateness traces back to March and Olsen 1989. See also March and Olsen 1998.
[22] See, for example, Brams 1980.

methodological individualism) is not of much practical use. Nor is the distinction between rational and appropriate behavior necessarily of much prescriptive value. Classical realism's call to statespeople to act rationally requires that those statespeople understand predominant norms of appropriate behavior in any given historical context, in order to be able to act in a strategically effective way.[23] Most realists would no doubt recognize, for example, that a use of weapons of mass destruction in the contemporary international system has implications beyond the immediate military effectiveness of the weapons. They are, in today's world, considered inappropriate.[24] An effective, rational strategy of foreign policy, therefore, requires that the social opprobrium attached to them be taken into account in calculating their utility as a tool of policy.

In other words, there are uses of the concept of rationality in the context of the study of international relations that do not position the concept in opposition to a logic of appropriateness. And it is likely that few constructivists would ultimately subscribe to a claim that the logic of appropriateness is the driving motive behind human behavior. After all, taken literally, the logic of appropriateness is as physiologically reductionist an assumption as the logic of strategic rationality. Both are based on claims that people behave a certain way because of the way their brains are hardwired – either for strategic thought or for social convention. In this sense an assumption of a logic of appropriateness is no more constructivist than the rational choice assumption of strategic logic.

Appropriateness and agency

The logic of appropriateness, then, is one that most constructivists would ultimately reject as a generalized assumption about human behavior. Used in a narrow sense logics of strategy and appropriateness are orthogonal to, rather than in opposition to, each other. Used in a broad sense, both are tautological, the claim of appropriate behavior no less so than the claim of rational behavior. Furthermore,

---

[23] Morgenthau 1967, pp. 6–8.
[24] On nuclear weapons, see Tannenwald 1999. On chemical weapons, see Legro 1995. On the social construction of "weapons of mass destruction" as a category, see Oren and Solomon 2008.

to assume that people will behave appropriately, according to social norms, comes very close to assuming that they are biologically hard-wired to do so. So to stress a logic of appropriateness is to be biologically materialist and biologically determinist in much the same way that some constructivists have accused both rationalists and realists of being. To get away from this determinism, one cannot assume *a priori* that people will behave either appropriately or strategically. One cannot, in fact, assume *a priori* that individuals will act in any specific way. One must allow for them to act in unpredicted ways, in ways that are different from how another individual might act. One must, in other words, grant them agency.[25]

And herein lies the greatest danger of definitions of constructivism that rely too much on the logic of appropriateness versus that of strategic thinking – they leave insufficient room for human agency. In this sense such a constructivism would be static, in much the same way that constructivists accuse realism, and particularly neorealism, of being static.[26] The criticism of neorealism is that, being a theory of structural continuity, it is unable to account for changes in structure.[27] But a focus on a logic of appropriateness is itself structural in ways analogical to the international system in neorealism. If people act according to existing social norms, and do not interact with those norms strategically, then where do the norms come from, and how do they change? In Wendt's terminology, how does one prevent a constructivism based on an assumption of the logic of appropriateness from being ontologically reducible to norms?[28]

Norms could presumably change in response to changing material conditions, much as there is change in the Waltzian neorealist system in response to a changed distribution of capabilities.[29] But that does not sound like a very constructivist answer. Absent of such external drivers of change, there is no mechanism for change within a social structure. Social conditions presumably could not be drivers of change, because given conditions are reproduced as people act in

---

[25] I am using the term "agency" here in a narrow sense, to mean purposive activity that is conceptually distinct from activity forced by structural constraints. This approach to agency is described in detail in Chapter 7 of this book. See also Klotz and Lynch 2007, Chapter 3.

[26] For example Wendt 1987.   [27] Ruggie 1983.

[28] This mirrors Wendt's 1987 argument that neorealism is ontologically reducible to states.

[29] Waltz 1979.

a set pattern of appropriateness. The only way social conditions can change independently of material conditions is for people either to challenge existing norms (i.e. not behave appropriately) or to deploy those norms strategically.[30] In other words, the only way for norms to change in a socially constructed world is through agency, and there is no room in a pure logic of appropriateness for agency.

The role of individual agency in both constructivism and realism is taken up again in Chapter 7. The key point here is that a logic of the social should not be conflated with a logic of appropriateness. People may well behave in a manner appropriate to social norms, but a logic of the social does not require that we assume that they do. A social constructivist approach to the study of international relations does indeed by definition require a focus on the social, but it cannot be ontologically reduced to the social – it cannot really be called constructivist if there is no construction going on, and the process of constructing international politics is undertaken by agents. Defining constructivism in opposition to rationalism, without stressing that the opposition is to the methodological individualism of rational choice theory rather than the idea that people use reason, risks missing the point.

The logic of the social

The logic of the social, then, should be seen as being in opposition to methodological individualism, rather than in opposition to rationality. It could even be called methodological socialism if that term did not imply something vaguely Stalinist. It is the idea that we cannot understand people, their identities, their interests, their discourses, or their behaviors, in isolation from their social context. This context, made up of intersubjectively held norms, rules, and discourses, not only defines the rules of interaction among people, but defines who those people see themselves to be in the first place. Social context provides the generative logic of political interaction, that enables rather than (or in addition to) constrains individual behavior. Constructivists often refer to this generative logic as constitutive rules and norms, as opposed to the regulatory rules and norms of liberal regime theory.[31]

---

[30] See, in this context, Finnemore 1996b, pp. 339–344.

[31] On constitutive rules and constitutive argument, see Dessler 1989, p. 455; and Wendt 1999, pp. 77–88. For a critique of the regulative/constitutive distinction, see Smith 2000.

Constructivism does not share its basis in the social with all other approaches to the study of international relations, but it does share this basis with some of them. For example, despite the tension between constructivism and some Marxist approaches (such as Leninist imperialism[32] or world systems theory[33]) on the subject of historicity, they share a common basis in the social. This may seem at first glance odd, given Marxism's self-description as materialist. But the ontological starting point of the Marxist approaches is the set of social relationships that together form relations of production. These relationships are economic rather than normative, but they are nonetheless fundamentally social, in that one cannot understand the relationships of production by aggregating up from the study of individual participants in the economy. To understand Marxist political economy you must start with inherently social units such as class, rather than with autonomous individuals.

Another approach to the study of international relations that shares with constructivism a basis in the logic of the social is realism. Once again, this may at first glance seem odd given realism's us-versus-them perspective.[34] But prior to the relationship between "us" and "them" is the constitution of "us." E. H. Carr, for example, noted that "[a]ll attempts to deduce the nature of society from the supposed behavior of man in isolation are purely theoretical, since there is no reason to assume that such a man has ever existed."[35] And realisms for the most part locate the "us" squarely in the institution of the modern state.[36] In assuming that states are the location of the capabilities that matter to international power politics, realists are also implicitly assuming that the state is a focus of both accepted authority and popular loyalties. Realists, in other words, need to assume that people will be willing to die for their state, a level of loyalty that people will not accord other social institutions (because if people are willing to accord that level of loyalty to other social institutions,

[32] Lenin 1969 [1917].   [33] Wallerstein 1974.
[34] Although it is interesting to note in this context that some constructivist scholarship also begins with the us-versus-them distinction. See, for example, Klotz and Lynch 2007, p. 74.
[35] Carr 1964, p. 95.
[36] Although different realists get there in different ways – Morgenthau 1967, pp. 97–105, for example, argues for the state as the relevant "us," whereas neorealists, such as Waltz 1979 and Mearsheimer 2001, tend simply to assume it.

these institutions in turn will become more powerful relative to the state).[37] Neorealists tend to bury this assumption by anthropomorphizing states as actors without questioning the source of their power over people. But the argument that states are more important than other actors in international politics draws clearly on the idea that states will be more successful in maintaining their condition as effective social organizations over the long term, and more effective in motivating their members to underwrite the power resources relevant to international relations. In other words, neorealists often assume individual affinity without deigning to recognize that assumptions about affinity are necessary.[38]

All three of these approaches – constructivism, Marxism, and realism – begin with assumptions of social affinity within groups. For realists the affinity is nationalist – they either assume that people will have a political affinity with others in the same country, or observe that in contemporary politics this is the case. When it is not the case, as when actors in international politics show a greater affinity with non-nationalist ideas such as religion or the environment, realists are often at a loss to explain patterns of international politics.[39] For classical Marxists the affinity is economic rather than nationalist. It is also objective, in the sense that one has a real affinity with one's class whether or not one realizes it, whether or not recognition of the affinity is affected by false consciousness.

The affinity in constructivism is less specified than in either realism or classical Marxism. It differs from the class affinity of Marxism, however, in that there is no "objective" affinity apart from those that are intersubjectively recognized. In other words, intersubjectivity is constitutive to constructivism analogically to the way in which relations of production are constitutive to classical Marxist theory. The affinity in constructivism, often discussed in terms of identity,[40] can

---

[37] Robert Jervis allows that this characterization of the centrality of the state is "descriptively inaccurate," but nonetheless yields a more accurate description of international politics than alternatives. Jervis 1998, p. 980.

[38] See, for example, Waltz 1979, pp. 93–96.

[39] In the case of the environment, the result is often the "securitizing" of the environment. See, *inter alia*, Deudney and Matthew 1999.

[40] For a discussion of issues surrounding the use of identity in constructivism, see *inter alia* Goff and Dunn 2004.

be national,[41] international[42] (as in the international society of the English school,[43] or norms of sovereignty across states[44]), or sub- or transnational.[45] A key difference, then, between the logics of the social in classical Marxism and constructivism is that the key social structures in the former are transhistorically given, and in the latter they are historically contingent and intersubjective. Different realist scholars fit into this categorization differently. Neorealists tend to be transhistorical in this sense in that they tend to assume nationalist affinity.[46] Classical realists often did not do so, and accepted both that nationalist affinity is contingent, and that the strength of this affinity was itself a factor in national power.[47]

The logic of the social in constructivism also differs from its equivalent in many Marxisms and realisms in that it is co-constitutional. One can have a logic of the social in which social structure is ontologically prior to the individual. A realism that assumes nationalist affinity would be one such approach. Some Marxisms similarly see class as prior to an agent–structure dialectic, although Marx's dictum that people make history, but not in circumstances of their choosing, suggests a role for the dialectic nonetheless. Nor need social reductionism be transhistorical, as is the case with a focus on class. The French school of structural Marxism sees the content of social structure as historically specific, but still begins with the study of the structure, without particularly allowing for the effects of agency on structure.[48]

Constructivism, on the other hand, looks both at the role of structure in creating agents, and the role of agents in creating and reproducing structure. This means in turn that the constructivist logic of the social does not take social structure simply as a given. It looks as well at the ways in which that structure is maintained through practice, and the ways in which the discourses, rules, and norms that

---

[41] Hopf 2002.
[42] For example, Adler and Barnett 1998; Wendt 1999.
[43] Bull 1977.   [44] Barkin and Cronin 1994; Barkin 1998.
[45] For example, Klotz 1995; Keck and Sikkink 1998; Cronin 1999.
[46] This is true, for example, of Waltz 1979; Gilpin 1981; and Mearsheimer 2001, all of whom assume the existence of a national interest (as opposed to individual or other group interests).
[47] See, for example, Carr 1964, pp. 226–231; Morgenthau 1967, pp. 122–132.
[48] See, for example, Althusser 1971.

constitute the structure can be deployed strategically by agents.[49] Studying social structure and human agency as a process of mutual constitution is what allows constructivist research to avoid the problem of stasis inherent in the logic of appropriateness, a problem shared with those approaches that assume social structure without allowing for recursive effects by agents on that structure.

Liberalism, deconstruction, and the social

The logic of the social thus underlies many approaches to the study of international relations, including both sociological approaches such as constructivism and political paradigms such as realism and Marxism. The specific logic generally used in constructivism is more precise, with its dialectic of structure and agent, than can be attributed to the social logics of realism and Marxism generally, given that different variants of the latter two adopt different logics of the social. This is not surprising, given that constructivism is social theory, in that it is about how we should understand social interaction, and therefore it should be expected to have a precise logic of the social. Realism and Marxism have as their core focus ideas of how politics and economic relations work, and therefore social theory is to them a secondary concern. In other words, specific approaches to the study of international relations that adopt somewhat different social theories can still fit within the same political paradigm as long as the common political theme is there. Even so, given the starting assumptions of both realism and Marxism it is difficult to see how there could be an approach to either that is not in some way based in a logic of the social.

Does this suggest that all approaches to the study of international relations except for rational choice theory share a logic of the social? In fact, several approaches, including in particular most strains of liberal theory, do not. This claim is worth elaborating upon, because much constructivist research seems sympathetic to some of the assumptions of liberal international relations theory.[50] The case that liberal international relations theory is incompatible with a logic of the social is relatively straightforward, because in key ways the common theme underlying the various strands of liberalism that underpin it is specifically their ontological individualism. This is the case whether one is

---

[49] Klotz and Lynch 2007.   [50] Sterling-Folker 2000; Barkin 2003a.

looking at utilitarian liberalisms, from which rational choice theory is descended, or rights-based liberalisms. In either approach, the social exists only as a set of contractual relationships among individuals, whether those relationships are designed to maximize utility or to protect individual rights. In other words, liberalism as a general approach privileges the rights or utility of individuals as logically prior to the social structure in which they find themselves, and a social structure that does not respect those rights is morally wrong.

This does not mean that constructivist methods cannot be used to study things like the diffusion of liberal norms, or cannot be motivated by politically liberal commitments on the part of the researcher. For that matter, the diffusion of liberal norms can be studied from realist or Marxist perspectives (or from a realist constructivist perspective, as I argue in the conclusion to this book). But as a method of studying international relations, any liberal constructivism will suffer from the tension between epistemology and ontology that Kratochwil and Ruggie ascribe to neo-utilitarian approaches.[51] In other words, a constructivist study of (for example) human rights would see those rights as historically contingent, whereas a liberal understanding of those rights would see them as transhistorical. Liberal constructivists need then to recognize that that their political commitment is itself part of a historical contingency. In other words, they need to be reflexive about their beliefs. A number of mainstream constructivists in the United States face this problem, but fail to address it explicitly.[52] Of course, any constructivist needs to be reflexive about his or her political beliefs, an issue that is discussed further in Chapter 6. But the problem is particularly acute for a liberal constructivism given the dominant place that liberal political theory holds in contemporary Western, and particularly American, society.

There is a tension as well between constructivism and deconstructive methods, for reasons that are in a way the opposite of the case with liberalism. Whereas the strong individualism of liberalism is in tension with a logic of the social, the absence of the independent subject in deconstruction creates a tension with the idea of intersubjectivity. Deconstruction is premised on the idea that there is no authoritative reading of text, and therefore there are no commonly and intersubjectively held meanings. There is no "social." Text, or discourse, in this

---

[51] Kratochwil and Ruggie 1986.   [52] Barkin 2003a.

sense creates subjectivity, but does not create intersubjectivity, to the extent that intersubjectivity is the common expression of discourse. The epistemic purpose of deconstruction, to examine difference in discourse, is in this sense distinct from the epistemic purpose of constructivism, to examine similarities across discourses.[53]

So what?

Constructivism is grounded in a logic of the social. It is a particular logic of the social, one that embraces agency and co-constitution as well as social structure. These particular features of the constructivist logic of the social are discussed in more detail in Chapters 6 and 7. More broadly, however, a general grounding in the logic of the social has often been used to distinguish constructivism from other approaches to the study of international relations, particularly rationalism. There are two key arguments developed in this chapter that follow from this particular understanding of the logic of the social, and that serve to more accurately place constructivism within the array of approaches to the study of international relations.

The first of these arguments is that rationalism is a tricky term to put in opposition to the logic of the social. As a description of an approach to social science that is rigidly methodologically individualist, the opposition is apposite. But the term "rationality" has other significantly different meanings, both in general parlance and in the context of other approaches to the study of international relations. As such, putting rationalism in opposition to the logic of the social implies differences that do not really exist between constructivist approaches and those that refer to rationality in non-methodologically individualist ways. One such approach is realism, at least in its pre-Waltzian forms.

The second key argument is that the opposition of constructivism with rationalism obscures the fact that there are approaches to the study of international relations that share with rational choice theory a methodological individualism, broadly defined, that do not rely on, and sometimes completely reject, the assumption of instrumental rationality, such as normative liberalisms. This observation suggests yet one more way in which dichotomizing the field of

[53] Zehfuss 2002 makes a similar point in her deconstruction of constructivism.

international relations as rationalists on the methodological right and social theorists on the methodological left, or presenting it as a tripartite realist/liberal/constructivist set of paradigms, is misleading and can be pedagogically counterproductive. Looking at methodological individualism and the logic of the social yields a set of divisions in the field that are quite different from those yielded by looking at, for example, the question of historical contingency.

These two arguments come together in what John Ruggie, in a key work of early constructivism (although it precedes the development of the term in international relations theory), calls "social purpose."[54] The idea of social purpose is clearly grounded in a logic of the social, implying as it does that a social group has, or expresses, a purpose that is in some way distinct from the accumulation of individual purposes within it. It is in this sense quite distinct from the methodological individualism of rational choice theory. But it commits neither to a logic of consequences nor a logic of appropriateness – it can encompass both, at the level of the social rather than at the level of the individual. It is not a particularly specific concept, especially insofar as it does not speak to the question of social agency, of whether we should study social institutions as if they were independent actors or rather focus on intersubjective understandings of those sharing a social purpose as expressed through individual agency. Both interpretations of social agency are compatible with constructivist logic, as will be discussed in the next chapter.

The concept of social purpose implies a public interest distinct from the private interests of the members of the public. It is this notion of a public interest, and its role in the relationship between constructivist and realist logic, that is the focus of the next chapter.

[54] Ruggie 1982.

5 | The public interest

Approaches to the study of international politics grounded in logics of the social require an idea of the social as political, an idea of social institutions as meaningful entities in the practice of politics apart from their role as institutional constraints on individual political actors. John Ruggie uses the term "social purpose" in this context to link constructivism with late nineteenth- and early twentieth-century Continental social theorists such as Durkheim and Weber.[1] Whether or not one accepts this particular understanding of the social as political, a social constructivist approach requires that one have some equivalent idea. Without such an idea one is left either with purely individualist motivations for political action, or without any source of change in political patterns and structures, which is to say without any politics at all. And even purely individualist motivations for individual action reflect social purpose, to the extent that individual identities and interests are socially constructed.

As I argue below, a common feature of constructivist ideas of the social as political is the concept of a public interest, defined as a set of political goals intersubjectively held within a social group, goals held for the group rather than (or as well as) for the members of the group as individuals. Any group of people whose political identity is, in whole or in part, focused on the group, and who hold common political goals for the group, have a public interest. This group can be, and in the context of international relations often is, congruent with the state, but it need not be. When it is, then the public interest becomes congruent with the national interest, creating a point of tangent between constructivist and realist logics. A discussion of the concept of the public interest is useful in locating constructivism and realism more clearly in the matrix of international relations theory, both in relation to each other and in relation to other approaches.

[1] Ruggie 1982 and 1983.

66

The concept of the public interest is used here in both an empirical and an intersubjective way. This is to be distinguished from normative arguments about what the public interest should be, or deductive arguments claiming an objective interest. This distinction, between on the one hand a concept of the public interest that is both empirical and intersubjective and on the other hand concepts of the public interest that are either normative or deductive, is an important one in this context. It points to a difference between those approaches to the study of international relations that look at the public interest as a historically contingent question, such as constructivism and realism as defined here, those that look at it transhistorically, those that look at it critically, and those approaches, ranging from liberalism to behavioralism, that aggregate private interests rather than recognizing a public one. The distinction is particularly important in establishing the relationship between constructivism and critical theory, as is discussed later in this chapter.

The distinction is also important because it suggests one of the key points of resonance between constructivist and realist theory. The national interest, an idea that is central to much realist thinking, is a particular public interest, and as such provides a point of contact between realism and constructivism. Being a public interest, the national interest is a social construct – it is intersubjective understandings that contribute content to the national interest, that give the state social purpose. Recognizing that the public interest is a social construct is all that stands between realism and what E. H. Carr called "an unreal kind of realism,"[2] by which he meant a realism without social purpose. This chapter begins with a discussion of the public interest, and then makes the case that this idea of a public interest is a key element in classical realist thinking.

The public interest

Constructivists look at rules, norms, and discourses that form the intersubjective understandings upon which social interaction is based. These discourses, rules, and norms at the same time constitute actors and are used by those actors to create and recreate social institutions. Constructivism as an approach to international relations looks

---

[2] Carr 1964, p. 235.

particularly at institutions that are relevant to international politics, broadly defined. Politics, as distinct from philosophy, say, or gardening, is an inherently social activity.[3] To engage in politics is to try to affect what the body politic as a whole does or does not do, can or cannot do. It is to try to affect what is done in the name of a social institution that itself has played a part in the construction of the political agents in question. This social institution can be anything that commands identity and affinity, be it a country, a non-governmental organization, or a political discourse ("democracy" or "emancipation," for example).

Politics is thus about trying to harness social institutions and drive them in a particular direction. Ruggie's phrase, "social purpose," in this sense is an inherent part of political activity – successful politics requires the moving of social institutions, and therefore the actors who constitute those institutions, to a purpose. That purpose can be moral – identifying activities that an institution that acts in one's name should or should not do, or it can be economic – an effort to use an institution to redistribute economic resources in one's favor. It can, in other words, be about appropriate or strategic behavior. But it will only be effective if it harnesses the activities and beliefs of other participants in the institution to the purpose. Social purpose is thus in a way a definitional feature of the *political* interaction of agent and structure in the construction of social institutions.

This purpose can be expressed in a number of ways. Specifically, it can be, but need not be, associated with corporate agency. The idea that social institutions, if endowed with characteristics like internal hierarchy, can act as agents is a commonplace one in the study of international relations, because the state is one of the institutions to which corporate agency is most commonly ascribed. The case that it is reasonable to think in terms of corporate agency within the constructivist approach to international relations, and more particularly to think of states as agents, with distinct social purposes, has been made, among others, by Christian Reus-Smit and Alex Wendt.[4] But social institutions do not need corporate agency in order to express a social purpose. Underlying political discourses, such as those involving terms like sovereignty, or human rights, or *jihad*, are social purposes, even if the discourses as social institutions do not embody agency.

---

[3] See, for example, Aristotle 1958.   [4] Reus-Smit 1999; Wendt 1999.

Social purpose in turn implies a public interest; "public" in the sense of a group of people identifying with a social institution.[5] When that institution is a country, the idea of a public is relatively straight-forward (Canadians, for example, constitute the public of the social institution that is Canada). But less hierarchical social institutions have publics as well. Political discourses have constituencies, people who identify themselves politically with the discourse. Actors who make use of that discourse are in effect co-opting the constituency, claiming them as a public. "Interest" in the sense simply that the public is interested, that the members of the relevant public have a concern, or a stake, in a particular issue. A public interest is thus the stake that a self-identifying group has in a political issue.[6] It is a slightly more specific concept than social purpose, in that "public" refers principally to the identity-constituting aspect of social institutions rather than to the corporate-agent aspect, and that "interest" is a more issue-specific concept than purpose. But it is also a key political manifestation of social purpose.

Two specifics of the way in which the concept of the public interest is being used here need to be stressed – that it is empirical and that it is intersubjective. It is empirical in the sense that a theory of the social construction of the political requires that there be a public interest, but does not specify what it is. The interest of a particular self-identifying public is historically contingent – we can attempt to find out what it is through research, but we cannot reasonably assume it *ex ante*. Nor, to the extent that it is an empirical rather than a normative approach, can a constructivist argument address the question of what the public interest *should* be. For example, a constructivist argument might be that a certain national public recognizes the internationalization of human rights norms as a public interest. A liberal theorist might argue that the same public should recognize the same norms in the same way. But these are two very different arguments.[7] The second argument, the normative one, may well be an exercise in social construction in the sense that it is designed to create a new intersubjective understanding of the public interest. But until such

[5] See, for example, Arendt 1958; Habermas 1991.
[6] On the sociological use of interest, see Swedberg 2005. The usage here is compatible with that in Bourdieu 1998.
[7] Although they can be made in the context of the same scholarship. See for example Keck and Sikkink 1998.

a discourse is broadly accepted within the self-identifying public, it does not constitute a public interest in the constructivist sense.

This suggests a clear distinction between liberal and constructivist approaches to the study of international relations, a distinction that is related to liberalism's methodological individualism discussed in the previous chapter. This applies both to normative liberalisms and utilitarian liberalisms, both of which ultimately posit a public interest that is an aggregate of individual interests. Being individual, they are not at base socially constructed – they either are (in utilitarian liberalism) or should be (in normative liberalism) prior to the social, and therefore not really public.[8]

The second specific way in which the concept of the public interest is being used here is that it is intersubjective. The public is whoever considers themselves to be the public, and the public interest is whatever they consider the public interest to be. If, for example, a group of balding people come to identify primarily with their follicular condition, rather than with a country, or ethnicity, or profession, and act politically to further the interests of balding people, then they are a public. If the same group of people choose not to identify with each other, then they would not have a public interest in the politics of balding. There are two ramifications of this specification. The first is that the public interest is not a material or transhistorical fact. There is no inherent public interest in, say, greater wealth, or greater levels of public participation, or conquest. There is not even an inherent public interest in state security and survival.[9] Any of these can feature in the public interest if the public as a whole recognizes it as such. And one can certainly make the case that some proximate capabilities (such as greater wealth, however measured) tend to enable a variety of potential public interests (which is different than saying that wealth is an ultimate interest in itself). But if the public intersubjectively believes that poverty is in the public interest, then that is the public interest – because the term as used in this constructivist sense is both empirical and intersubjective, what the public thinks is in its interest is the public interest, by definition. The public cannot, in this sense, be wrong (although it can be wrong

[8] See, for example, Rawls 1971.
[9] This latter assumption is fundamental to neorealism. See, for example, Waltz 1979.

in its strategic calculations of the relationship between proximate capabilities and ultimate interests).

A related observation, and the second ramification of intersubjectivity in this context, is that the public is whoever the public considers themselves to be. The national interest is a public interest inasmuch as the citizens of a state identify with the state, and recognize a national interest in common.[10] To the extent that a group of people identify with a non-state social group, such as a religion, an ethnicity, a social movement, or some other social identifier, and that group shares a set of political preferences or norms, or a common political language, then that group has a public interest associated with the identity its members hold in common. This can be the case at the global level as well. To the extent that practitioners of international politics speak a common political discourse and hold common political goals for the international system, then there is an international public interest.[11] But public in this instance refers to the self-identifying community of participants in traditional interstate politics, and may well not be a public interest for the global population more broadly.[12]

One possible self-identifying group is a social class. From a constructivist perspective, however, a class interest exists only insofar as people with similar socioeconomic characteristics (or who see themselves as having similar socioeconomic characteristics) identify with each other politically rather than, or in addition to, other forms of identification. As is the case with nationalism, class identification is historically contingent. In this sense, approaches to Marxism that speak of class as an objective category are not compatible with constructivist analysis – class exists as a social construct only insofar as people identify themselves with class. Traditional Marxisms, in this sense, do use a concept of public interest, but identify that interest transhistorically with class. This use of the concept, as is the case

[10] Note that this use of the term "national interest" is somewhat different from that in Krasner 1978. He is really talking about the state interest, the observed interests of the state as a corporate actor, rather than of the national public. This state interest is still a public interest, but the relevant public is the state as a corporation, rather than the nation as a self-identifying social group.

[11] See, for example, Ellis 2005 and 2009.

[12] This definition of an international public interest is roughly compatible with the concept of "international society" as used by the English school of international relations theory. See, for example, Bull 1977.

with many normative liberal approaches to the study of politics, is distinct from the intersubjective and empirical status of the concept in constructivist logic.

Given that realists focus primarily on the state, and often assume that the state is the social structure with which people identify politically, it would seem at first glance that the public interest should be understood by constructivists in a manner that is distinct from realism in a way analogous to the manner in which it is distinct from Marxism. After all, realists in a way simply replace class interest with national interest. And then define that interest in terms of power politics.[13] But the assumption of the state in classical realism should not be taken too far – it is, as noted in Chapter 2, an empirical observation, not a transhistorical claim. And power is only a proximate interest, a means to political ends – a realism that does not address those ultimate political ends can say little about international politics.

Interest and utopia

The two issues that would seem to come between the constructivist and the realist logics of the social, then, are the focus on the state as a locus of identity and the focus on power politics as the content of its interest. The realist focus on the state (and the resultant focus on the national interest as the key form of public interest) in the end derives from the state's power. Empirical observation of power elsewhere in the international system should get a reasonable realist (and to be unreasonable, *pace* Morgenthau, is to not be a realist) to be concerned with the public interest, whether it be the social purpose or the corporate interest, of the group with the power. The key tension between constructivist and realist logic in this context, then, comes down to the transhistoricity of power as interest.

But the classical realists were specifically arguing against transhistoricity. For them, power politics itself is simply a means to an end. Classical realists saw power not as a transhistorical interest *per se*, but as a definitional element of politics. By this understanding, power is to politics as wealth is to economics.[14] Power politics in this sense is the ability to achieve your public interest in a world in which it is in conflict with other public interests. But one still needs a public

---

[13] Morgenthau 1967, p. 5.   [14] Morgenthau 1967, pp. 5, 15–17.

interest in order for national power to have purpose. When scholars such as Carr and Morgenthau argued for an association of interest with power politics, they were arguing against the idea that one could impute interests across time, and for the idea that those interests are historically contingent.

As rhetorical foils to realism, E. H. Carr used "utopianism" and Hans Morgenthau used "liberalism" and "scientific man."[15] Although the terms that Carr and Morgenthau employed seem quite different, both were, in fact, referring to the sort of liberal idealism and scientific humanism often associated with political scientists in the tradition of Woodrow Wilson.[16] The essence of this school of thought is that people have consistent and reasonable (or at least predictable) preferences, which they pursue rationally.[17] As a result, well-designed political institutions within which people can rationally pursue their preferences in a way that interferes as little as possible with the abilities of others to do so will appeal sufficiently to people's reasonableness as to obviate any necessity for power politics. In other words, for the liberal idealist the right political structure can, indeed, insure perpetual peace (to use Immanuel Kant's phrase[18]). But for the realist, political institutions, no matter how well designed, can never eliminate power politics. And for the classical realist power politics is contextual, subject to the conditions of time and place. Faith in political structures is misplaced even if those structures seem to work well under particular conditions, because conditions will necessarily change. And when they do, institutional adjustment will follow political power.

So, then, is there ultimately nothing other than power politics that matters in international relations? Quite the contrary. Classical realists tended to speak of morality rather than norms or social rules, but the thrust of the argument remains the same. The difference in terminology can to a large extent be ascribed to the difference between

---

[15] Carr 1964; Morgenthau 1946.   [16] See Kegley 1993; Schmidt 1998.
[17] A key difference between this school of thought and contemporary rationalist approaches in the study of IR is that in the latter the assumption of reasonableness falls out. People are assumed to be instrumentally rational, but are not necessarily assumed to respect the rights and well-being of others when to do so would not be demonstrably instrumentally rational.
[18] Kant 1957.

constructivism's grounding in explanation and realism's grounding in prescription. The former leads to the more generic discourse of norms, ways in which people (generally other people) feel they should behave. The latter leads to the more specific discourse of morality, the way in which we believe we should behave in matters of high politics and foreign policy. In this context, then, the realist category of morality can be understood as a subset of the constructivist category of norms.[19] And morality is something that was of central concern to the classical realists.

For Morgenthau, for example, people are inherently moral as well as political animals; all political acts have ethical significance.[20] For Carr, "it is an unreal kind of realism which ignores the element of morality in any world order."[21] In classical realism, moral theory, the assertion of political norms, in the absence of a recognition of power is a futile exercise. But the use of power in the absence of morality is an empty exercise. The latter is the case for two reasons, one practical and one philosophical. The practical reason is that, because humans are moral beings, they will not accept power without morality. The subjects of political domination recognize the distinction we are trying to make here: between power used for good and power used for evil. And they support the former and oppose the latter.[22] The philosophical reason is that power for its own sake is hollow; it gets you nowhere without some notion as to what to do with it. Indeed, "the characteristic vice of the utopian is naivete; of the realist, sterility."[23] Classical realists, thus, viewed the art of international politics as the practical balancing of the demands of power on the one hand and morality on the other – as a dialectic between power and morality.[24]

In other words, for realists (or at least for the classical realist) a recognition of the public interest is not by itself a sufficient basis for policy prescription, but is a necessary basis. The logic of realism, in

[19] That political morality is a subset of the thick constructivist category of discourse is even more straightforward, in the sense that political morality is a discursive construction.

[20] Morgenthau 1946, pp. 177–178.   [21] Carr 1964, p. 235.

[22] See, for example, Morgenthau 1946, pp. 176–178, and the discussion of Thucydides in Johnson Bagby 1994.

[23] Carr 1964, p. 12.

[24] This point has been made by several scholars recently. See, for example, Rosenthal 1991; Murray 1997; Kubálková 1998; and Williams 2005.

other words, needs a public interest. Furthermore, by the same logic, there is a recognition that there are other public interests held by other publics, and that these interests must be understood in order to prescribe effective policy. Finally, classical realists recognized that these interests are historically contingent. In this latter sense, the constructivist and realist concepts of the public interest are compatible in a way that neither are with conceptions of interest in liberalism or classical Marxism.

Power politics and the public interest

Those critical theorists who have made it thus far into this chapter have no doubt been cringing at the repeated use of the phrase "public interest." For critical theorists the concept of a public interest is more likely to be associated with a social power structure than with a benign reading of the collective good. From a critical perspective, the concept of a public interest is a mechanism through which the power structure is maintained. It is a way in which individuals are convinced to reproduce existing power structures through practice, by denying a voice to those for whom the public interest does not speak.[25] People accept a common understanding of the public good, act according to that understanding in a way that reinforces existing social structures, which in turn reinforce the understanding of what constitutes the public good. Discourses of national security provide a useful example of this difference. Realists see a national security discourse as a way to establish the most effective manner of defending a country from external threats. Critical theorists see it as a way to reinforce the domestic position of a national security elite by generating a fear of the foreign.[26] For realists, power politics are the means to achieve the public good. For critical theorists, the public good is a means to maintain power.

At one level, classical realists recognized the critical reading of power politics and public interest. E. H. Carr, for example, noted that for a statesperson, the claim of a national interest is a way of "clothing his own interest in the guise of a universal interest for the

[25] See, for example, George 1989 and 1994.
[26] For a constructivist analysis of security that speaks to both of these positions, see Buzan, Waever, and de Wilde 1998.

purpose of imposing it on the rest of the world."[27] In other words, what may seem to us as an action that promotes the global public good may well be seen by others as an effort to maintain our place in the global power structure. This suggests a certain compatibility between classical realism and critical theory.[28] This compatibility is further suggested by a common discourse of power. Both realists and critical theorists speak of power not only as a common feature of international politics, but as a definitional feature of politics more generally. And for both, avoiding being subject to power is a key concern.

But at another level, the realist and critical theory readings of the concept of the public interest betray a different understanding of power (hence the use of the term "power politics" in this volume to express the realist understanding of power, to avoid confusion). At its most simple, the difference is this: realists understand power to be relational,[29] while critical theorists understand power to be structural as well. Relational power is the power of one actor over another. Structural power "inheres in structures and discourses that are not possessed and controlled by any single actor."[30] For the realist, a discourse about the public interest underpins the use of state power. For the critical theorist, that discourse is itself what empowers the state as a social structure. Arguments can be made in favor of one or the other of these interpretations of power.[31] Ultimately, it is not clear whether it is possible (or, for that matter, necessary or desirable) to reconcile the relational and critical understandings of power.[32] It may make more sense to look at them as different, although related, concepts that share the same word.

Both the realist and the critical understanding of power, as power politics and as social structure, are compatible with constructivist approaches to the study of international relations. A constructivist can recognize that discourses, rules, and norms can be deployed (either strategically or habitually) by individuals to maximize interests with

---

[27] Carr 1964, p. 75.
[28] See, for example, Linklater 1997; Kubálková, Onuf, and Kowert 1998.
[29] Guzzini 1993.   [30] Barnett and Duvall 2005, p. 44.
[31] Guzzini 1993; Barnett and Duvall 2005.
[32] Sterling-Folker and Shinko 2005. See Jackson and Nexon 2004 for the argument that a realist constructivism requires a critical understanding of power.

respect to other individuals or groups.[33] At the same time, the constructivist can recognize that discourses and rule- and norm-governed behavior often have the effect of recreating the social structures in which they are embedded, and as such constrain actors and keep them subject to those same structures. And constructivists can recognize how theorizing about relational power and social structure can have the recursive effect of creating both that structure and those forms of relational power, how in this sense theory creates reality rather than responding to it.[34]

A critical public interest?

So can constructivism then be seen as a bridge between realist and critical theory, by spanning both understandings of power? No, it cannot, because there remains a key distinction between the way critical theory on the one hand and both realism and constructivism on the other view the concept of the public interest. This distinction can be summed up in the word "emancipation."

Emancipation is a key concern of critical theory. The focus on emancipation is, along with the centrality of structural power and the generative role of theory, arguably a core element of critical theory as an approach to the study of international relations.[35] Critical theory focuses on the place of the individual within a social structure, be that structure defined economically or discursively, and emancipation in this context therefore refers to emancipation from that power inherent in that social structure. Emancipation, in other words, means freeing the individual from the power structure, rather than working within that structure to maximize interest.[36]

The realist worldview, on the other hand, focuses not on the power structures constraining (and defining) individuals within a social group, but on relations among social groups. An assumption underlying realist theory is that we either cannot or choose not to remove ourselves, as a group represented by a state, from international politics.

---

[33] For a discussion of this focused on discourse and representation, see Mattern 2005a and 2005b.
[34] Guzzini 2005.   [35] Linklater 1992; Brown 1994; Wyn Jones 2001.
[36] E.g. Booth 1991. The description here is of course a gross simplification of a broad corpus of work, but the centrality of emancipatory purpose is to be found across critical theoretical approaches.

Therefore, realist international relations theory is about maximizing the political power of our social group relative to that of others. The concept of personal emancipation can gain no traction both because realism is a theory of social units rather than of individuals, and because our power is relational to that of others – we either cannot be or choose not to be free of it. Because the focus is on relational power (the relationship of the power of one group to that of another), realism looks to improve the balance of power (ours relative to theirs, whoever 'they' may be) rather than to escape it.

Because of the critical theory focus on the place of the individual within a social structure, and on emancipation from that structure, however, the symmetry of power relations to be found in realist analysis (confrontations among social groups) is replaced by an asymmetrical relationship between the individual and society. This asymmetry in turn can be traced back to a structural as well as relational understanding of power – since structural power in part defines the social structure, one can change it only by changing the social structure. The individual can become more or less free of social power, but cannot in any meaningful way balance against it, because of this inherent asymmetry of the individual–social relationship. Hence a focus on emancipation rather than on balancing.

This distinction between balancing and emancipation signifies a key difference between realist logic on the one hand and emancipatory theory on the other, be the emancipatory theory critical or of another variety (and other bases for emancipatory theory range from liberalism to religion). This is a difference of political purpose. Critical theory looks to emancipation from power structures. Realist theory looks to effective use of power structures (although the phrase "power structure" has a somewhat different meaning in the two usages). Realism in this sense is politically conservative, in the small-c sense of the term. It looks to the maintenance of one's position within a power structure, rather than withdrawal from, or radical transformation of, that structure. It is, in other words, a theory of the politics of small change rather than the politics of great change. This political tension inheres regardless of differences in method or of epistemology, and is more fundamental than can be bridged by constructivism.

But the constructivist approach to the study of international relations has its own tensions with the concept of emancipation, albeit different tensions than those of realism. Put simply, the constructivist logic of the social does not allow for the emancipation of the individual from social structures. Without the social, there is no individual in any meaningful way, because the individual and the social are co-constitutive. And constructivist logic does not inherently privilege particular social constructions over others. Constructivism is in this sense not a normative theory of politics in the same way that realism and critical theory are, but an empirical social theory – it is about how social relations in general do work, not how politics should work.[37] In other words, there is no normative political prescription inherent to constructivism, in the way that there is for both critical theory (the individual should be emancipated) and realism (the state should be acting in the national interest).[38]

Critical theorists, then, are likely to be uncomfortable with the idea of a public interest for reasons similar to those that make the public interest a core concept for constructivism. For both constructivists and critical theorists, a public interest is constitutive of the conduct of politics. In constructivist logic the public interest is constitutive of individuals as political actors, while for critical theorists it is more likely to be a mechanism for political subjugation, unless it is specifically emancipatory. It is an effective mechanism specifically because, once again, it is constitutive of individuals as political actors. One difference between these two approaches is, as noted above, the degree to which emancipation from constitutive public interests is possible. Another, and related, difference is in the role of theory in the study of politics.

Constructivism as social theory is to an important degree an inductive exercise, one concerned with empirical research into the normative and discursive basis of social interaction. This is the case whether one practices a neoclassical or postmodern constructivism, and whether or not one subscribes to the scientific/philosophic realist variant of the approach.[39] Whether looking for the "real" normative structure of international politics, or eschewing the idea of a "real" social structure and looking instead at discursive patterns,

---

[37] Onuf 1989; Wendt 1999.

[38] The absence of normative commitment is why some critical theorists in international relations are less than enthusiastic about constructivism. See, for example, Murphy 2007. See as well Hoffmann 2009.

[39] On scientific/philosophical realism and constructivism, see Wendt 1999; Patomäki and Wight 2000.

constructivists generally agree that what they are trying to do is to find out what the intersubjective patterns underlying particular political processes are, how those patterns have been created, and how they are reproduced.[40] As is discussed in the next chapter, internally consistent constructivism needs to do this reflexively, but this reflexiveness remains grounded in induction.

Critical theory as social theory, however, is grounded in a very different understanding of reflexivity.[41] A premise of many approaches to critical theory is that empirics cannot be divorced from theory as a matter of ontology as well as a matter of epistemology.[42] This means that for the critical theorist, the purpose of theory is emancipatory rather than empirical. The purpose of theory, in other words, is not to provide an explanation or an understanding of how the world works, but a vehicle for changing it. This does not at all mean that critical theorists are uninterested in understanding how the world works. Rather, it means that in this approach political theory is ontologically prior to, and epistemologically inseparable from, the empirical observation of the conduct of politics. However similar the approaches to empirical evidence of many constructivist and critical approaches may be, the former is more fundamentally an empirical approach to the study of politics than the latter. For the former, in other words, the public interest is an observation; for the latter, a political tool.[43]

So what?

In constructivist logic, interests are socially constructed, rather than exogenously given. Being social constructs, those interests are in turn social, rather than purely individual. To the extent that those interests are shared within an identity group, and form the basis for political interaction, either within the identity group or between groups,

---

[40] Finnemore and Sikkink 1998; Klotz and Lynch 2007.

[41] Critical theory as social theory refers to critical theory's epistemological stance that theory (the lens through which we see the world) cannot be separated from perceived reality (the world that we see). This is in distinction to critical theory as political theory, with its focus on emancipation.

[42] Cox 1986.

[43] For the argument that the distinction between constructivism and critical theory is not as distinct as I make it out to be, see Price and Reus-Smit 1998; and Reus-Smit 2001a.

they constitute a public interest. Constructivism as an approach to the study of politics, therefore, assumes that there will be some kind of public interest, as an empirical observation. The existence of a public interest, from a constructivist perspective, is an inductive rather than a normative claim – it is a starting point of politics, rather than something to be achieved or from which to be emancipated.

This position with respect to the concept of the public interest distinguishes constructivism from other approaches to the study of international relations. It distinguishes it from individualist approaches, be they methodologically or normatively individualist, by positing a public interest that is conceptually distinct from individual interests. It distinguishes constructivism from approaches that focus *ex ante* on particular group identities and thereby look primarily at a circumscribed set of public interests, as realism does with its focus on national identity and the national interest. And it distinguishes between primarily inductive approaches to the public interest such as constructivism and primarily normative understandings of the public interest, as is the case with critical theory.

The two particular relationships to constructivism to be stressed in this context are those with critical theory on the one hand and realism on the other. The relationship with critical theory is worth stressing because it is easy to see constructivism and critical theory as closely related and compatible approaches to the study of international relations. In fact, some discussions of constructivism by practitioners imply that the two are compatible, that constructivism is just a little more research-oriented.[44] But there are important ontological and epistemological distinctions between the two approaches, even when they use similar research methods. These distinctions hold across the neoclassical/postmodern divide within constructivism. To neglect these distinctions does justice to neither approach.

The relationship with realism is worth stressing because, although the range of public interests that realists look at is constrained, the core idea of an empirical public interest is largely compatible with constructivist logic. Looking at the realist concept of the public interest through a constructivist lens is therefore both an ontologically and a methodologically reasonable exercise, and one that can provide useful service to realist analysis. It can do so by reminding realists that there

[44] Hopf 1998; Price and Reus-Smit 1998; Jacobsen 2003.

can be public interests other than the national interest that need to be taken into account in the study of international politics. This is true abroad, where assuming that core identities are necessarily national, and that national identities necessarily map onto national interests, can lead to serious foreign policy mistakes. It is also true domestically – the question of what a citizenry will support as a national interest can be answered only by looking at its discourses and rules. To assume a national interest deductively that is not intersubjectively shared can undermine the effectiveness of policy.

Looking at the concept of public interest through a constructivist lens can also serve to remind realists of the role of what Morgenthau called morality in realist theory. The public interest, whether it is a national interest or the collective interest of some other group, must have some purposive content. Without purposive content, without an intersubjective public morality, realist power politics is pointless. The same logic of the social that allows realists to speak of a national interest also limits the degree to which realists can reasonably speak of power politics for its own sake. The logic of the social, in other words, places constraints on those approaches to the study of international relations that are grounded in it. These constraints are the topic of the next chapter, beginning with constraints on the discussion of power for its own sake.

6 | *The constraints of the social*

A basis in the logic of the social, beyond its association with the concept of the public interest, has a number of other ramifications for approaches to the study of international relations. This basis, combined with an acceptance of historical contingency, allows one to use an approach as a lens through which to look at the social bases of international politics, and the processes of social construction and change of those politics, in a way that is impossible otherwise. Both constructivism and classical realism meet these conditions, and as a result display this potential to help us understand international politics. But the combination of the logic of the social and of historical contingency also places constraints on what can be done with these approaches, by forcing scholars who use them to accept that social constructions matter, that they differ across identity groups and other social entities (in turn complicated by the fact that identity groups overlap), and that they change over time.

Among these constraints are the need to contextualize power, the need for reflexivity, and the need for research methods that are both social and contextual. These three constraints can all be deduced through similar reasoning, which involves the application of the logics of the social and of historical contingency to specific questions of ontology, epistemology, and methodology.[1] The reasoning in all three cases focuses on a combination of intersubjectivity and historicity. Intersubjectivity in this context means that the use of the concept of power, the approach to reflexivity, and the methodological demands of both constructivist and classical realist logic all need to be understood in ways that focus on mutual understandings and common discourses among actors, rather than on individual understandings and individual readings of text. Historicity in this context means that

---

[1] On these distinctions in the context of the study of international relations, see Kratochwil and Ruggie 1986.

these three constraints limit the degree to which both constructivists and realists can generalize, and also limit the extent to which both can reasonably speak in absolutes.

The term "reasonably" as used in this context is carefully chosen. It is used not in the instrumentally rational sense of rational choice theory, but in a more colloquial sense, indicating thoughtfulness and appropriateness.[2] Doing research that looks at processes of social construction in a historically contingent way requires, for want of a better term, reasonableness. It requires, for example, a recognition that boundaries, among both social groups and historical contexts, are imprecise. A recognition that there is no precise ratio or threshold at which a norm can be considered intersubjectively held, no specific number of iterations beyond which a discourse becomes constitutional of politics.[3] Determining these things requires reasoned argument on the part of the researcher, and an open but critical mind on the part of the reader. In this sense, the requirements of this sort of research are the opposite of those of statistical analysis, which requires clear and explicit categorization.[4]

Reasonableness also needs to be applied to concepts such as power and reflexivity, and to questions of method. Fetishizing these concepts, or fetishizing questions of method, undermines our ability to study politics inductively, by prioritizing concept or method over empirics. By fetishizing I mean focusing on power, or reflexivity, or method as an end in itself, rather than as something that is important to take into account in the study of international relations insofar as it illuminates the politics that are the ultimate point of the study.[5] It is the difference between arguing that something matters, and arguing that only that thing matters. For example, to argue that power is a common feature of politics is a reasonable observation. It can even be a definitional statement – Morgenthau, for example, defines politics as the realm of social power.[6] But to argue that only power matters is

---

[2] Reasonableness used in this sense can draw on precedents as varied as Morgenthau 1948 and Habermas 1984.
[3] Klotz and Lynch 2007; Klotz and Prakash 2008.
[4] Also this should not be taken as an argument that statistical methods are incompatible with constructivism, a question that will be taken up again later in this chapter.
[5] On fetishizing method, see Barkin 2008.
[6] Morgenthau 1967.

different, because to do so is to argue that other things do not matter, and this is a much more difficult argument to make. Morgenthau, to continue with the example, spoke of peace as the ultimate goal.[7] Whether or not one agrees with this goal, to state it is clearly an admission that something matters in politics beyond power.

The limits of power

Power has already been discussed in a number of places in this book. A focus on power politics has been presented as the central feature of political realism, and the way in which realists understand power politics has been contrasted with broader ways of understanding power, including the idea of structural power as understood by critical theorists. But the use of the concept of power as an explanation of political patterns is inherently limited, in the same way that any other explanatory concept is limited, by the standard paradox of explanations, that if they explain everything in general then they cannot explain anything in particular.[8] In this sense, if power is invoked to explain everything in general, then it cannot be used to distinguish among individual events. Furthermore, the invocation of power as an ultimate goal of politics presents a sort of logical impossibility – if power is the ability to get what one wants, but all that one wants is power, how does one know if one has it? There must, as the classical realists point out, be some other goal, some other content to interests or goals beyond power itself, to make power politics a meaningful concept.[9] Finally, these two uses of the concept of power politics, as empirical explanation and as political goal, are distinct but are often conflated.[10]

Two particular examples serve to illustrate uses of the concept of power in the study of politics that do not fit well within the circumscribed understanding of power demanded by the logics of the social

---

[7] In fact, in the title of his best-known work "power" and "peace" share equal placement. Morgenthau 1967.

[8] Hacking 1999 uses this same paradox to make the argument that the study of social construction in social science is not useful.

[9] This idea is discussed in more detail both later in this chapter, and in Chapter 8.

[10] See, for example, Mearsheimer 2001, in which, in an exercise in circular logic, he argues that power should be the core interest of great powers because it is, and is the core interest because it should be.

and of historicity. The first of these examples fetishizes power as an ultimate goal in itself, while the second universalizes power as explanation. These examples are drawn from the work of Carl Schmitt and Kenneth Waltz respectively.

Carl Schmitt develops a theory of the political as oppositional. Politics, for him, is about friends and enemies, and therefore about winning and losing. Political power, as such, does not serve other normative purposes, as it does for the classical realists.[11] The goals of politics, and of political power, therefore, are self-referential – political power is about winning, not about getting what one wants, or having one's interests fulfilled, because there are no interests beyond winning. This concept of the political is social, in the sense that it is premised on the willingness of individuals to sacrifice themselves for the greater good of the polity. But it is social in a way that does not admit a public interest, beyond the crude dichotomy of friend and foe. It is also transhistorical, because it defines *ex ante* what politics are about, what the goals of political actors are or should be, as ontological condition rather than as historical artifact. For Schmitt, any thinking about political power that does not demand a duality of friend and foe is not only analytically misguided, it is normatively flawed.

Waltz's concept of power politics is much less explicitly normative. It does not make the claim that maximizing power should be the goal of states. In fact, Waltz argues explicitly that states *should not* let power "become the end they pursue."[12] (In this, he differs from offensive realists, such as John Mearsheimer, who argue that as an empirical matter, states are power maximizers.[13]) For Waltz, the goal of states both is and should be survival, and power politics should be used as a means to that end, rather than as an end in itself. States act to ensure their own survival by balancing the power of others. Power politics is thus secondary to survival as a goal of states, and a state's behavior with respect to power politics is determined by the demands of survival.

These two examples share the common feature that they use the concept of power politics in a sufficiently all-encompassing way that

---

[11] Schmitt 1976. For discussions of Schmitt's relationship with Morgenthau, see Pichler 1998 and Scheuerman 2007a. Morgenthau, as a student of Schmitt's, clearly drew on his thinking, but developed a much more nuanced view of the relationship between power and political morality.

[12] Waltz 1979, p. 126.   [13] Mearsheimer 2001.

it is not particularly useful to an inductive study of the contextual and social construction of international politics. In particular, they do so by associating a particular normative content, and a single normative goal, with their discussion of power politics. These goals differ significantly, being survival in the case of Waltz and domination in the case of Schmitt (although in the end both may come to the same thing, inasmuch as Schmitt sees domination as the sole route to survival). But the goals are imputed rather than observed, meaning that they are transhistorical rather than historically contingent, and they are individual rather than intersubjective. This makes them examples of the use of the concept of power that are incompatible with constructivist logic. But it also makes both examples of the use of the concept that are incompatible with classical realism, in particular with the claim that "[r]ealism does not define its key concept of interest defined as power with a meaning that is fixed once and for all."[14]

The claim that Waltz's use of the concept of power politics is incompatible with realist logic may seem at first glance misplaced. It is in part a semantic game – to the extent that international relations scholars consider Waltz to be the definitional realist, his use of the concept of power is by definition realist. But Waltz, in making his argument for a structural realism, was also making an argument against classical realism. That argument was based on a rejection of "reductionism."[15] Political morality and any specific content to the national interest is, by his definition, reductionist. Any social purpose is reductionist. As such, Waltz's use of the concept of power politics is specifically intended to be incompatible with that in classical realism.[16] Waltz does this to create a theory of system stability in international relations; he insists that his is not a theory of foreign policy. Whether or not it is a useful theory of system stability is certainly open to question, but this is not a question that will be pursued here. The point to be made here is that, as he insists, it cannot be a theory of foreign policy, as is classical realism, because foreign policy requires a content to power, a social purpose, and Waltz does not allow for such purpose.[17]

---

[14] Morgenthau 1967, p. 8. For the argument that Morgenthau specifically argued against Schmitt's theory of the political, see Scheuerman 2007b.

[15] Waltz 1979, pp. 60–67.

[16] Waltz 1979. See also Waltz 1959, where he makes his case against classical realism more directly.

[17] See, for example, Waltz 1986.

Reflexivity

An approach to the study of international relations that combines a focus on power politics with a logic of the social and a recognition of historical contingency, then, must be constrained by the recognition that power is both social and contingent. A broader constraint on any such approach is reflexivity, which is in turn necessary to the effective use of power analysis as policy prescription. In other words, it is necessary for any realism that is a theory of foreign policy (and I shall argue later on that any realism that is true to the core insight of the classical realists will be a theory of foreign policy). That reflexivity is a requirement of constructivism, if it is to be done well, is relatively non-contentious. The case for reflexivity in constructivism has been made well elsewhere,[18] and is reviewed only briefly here. The case for reflexivity in realism has also been made a number of times recently, so much so that the literature has been referred to as "reflexive" realism.[19] The case has also been made more broadly that the study of international relations in general, and the study of IR in the United States specifically, needs to be more reflexive.[20] The argument made here is not so broad, and is much more specific. It is that not only is the need for reflexivity a point of agreement between constructivism and any realism that has a social understanding of power, but that this need is constrained by the demands of reasonableness, in much the same way as is the social and contextual study of power.

Reflexivity can be thought of as an "awareness of the inherent limits and ambiguities" of one's approach.[21] It entails a recognition that one's analysis will inherently be biased to one's own perspective, because that is the only perspective one can really know, and that one cannot claim certainty in the estimation of the thinking of adversaries or counterparties. It also entails a recognition that, whether or not one aspires to value-neutrality (or objectivity) in one's research, one cannot attain it. As such, one should be self-conscious about the values that one is reading into one's political analysis.

---

[18] Guzzini 2000.
[19] The term is from Steele 2007, fn. 10. Steele includes in this literature Lang 2002; Lebow 2003; and Williams 2005.
[20] See, for example, Smith 2002.   [21] Guzzini 2000, p. 151.

Stefano Guzzini makes the argument that constructivism without reflexivity is either theoretically incoherent or redundant.[22] Put simply, constructivism sees political categories, both in terms of ideas and of political institutions, as socially constructed, and focuses on the empirical study of those ideas and institutions. Constructivists must therefore recognize that their own categorization of ideas and institutions (which they must have, because empirical information without categories is infinite) are also socially constructed, and that they are studying social constructions through the lens of other social constructions. To not recognize this is to be logically incoherent. Robert Keohane makes the same point in describing the alternative to rationalist theorizing as "reflectivist."[23]

Classical realism is no less constrained by the need for reflexivity. Reflexivity is, in a sense, a form of prudence (as applied to analysis rather than to policy recommendation), and prudence, as is discussed at greater length in Chapter 8, is a core value of classical realism. The proximate reason for the need in realism's case is driven by the need to understand the public interest, the intersubjective structure of political discourse and social purpose, in other countries, if policy prescriptions are to be effective. This contrasts with the equivalent proximate reason in the case of constructivism, which is driven more by claims of intellectual honesty and the needs of inductive method in the realm of the social. But the need in the case of both approaches is rooted in similar ontologies, in the acceptance by both approaches that there is no objective ideal to which all participants in international relations will agree to consistently over time.

The classical realists recognized a need for reflexivity.[24] Carr, for example, noted that "realism itself, if we attack it with its own weapons, often turns out in practice to be just as much conditioned as any other mode of thought. In politics, the belief that certain facts are unalterable or certain trends irresistible commonly reflects a lack of desire to change or resist them."[25] This observation is oddly similar to the critical theory response to realism, that the discourses of sovereignty, anarchy, and power politics are themselves what make international politics a realm of conflict and war.[26] This recursiveness

---

[22] Guzzini 2000, p. 148.   [23] Keohane 1988.
[24] Williams 2005 makes this case at length with respect to Morgenthau's work.
[25] Carr 1964, p. 89.   [26] Walker 1987 and 1993.

is unavoidable in social science, insofar as the ultimate objects of study in social science can read it, and change their behavior based on it (whether the change is for strategic or normative reasons). But reflexivity provides a useful check on this recursiveness, and limits the extent to which realism can become its own unchecked feedback loop of power competition.[27]

Beyond this recursiveness, realism needs to be reflexive because the core realist argument, that we must take power seriously in studying international relations, requires reflexive analysis. Realism as a theory of foreign policy also requires that we take questions of political morality seriously, and this in turn requires reflexivity as well. And finally, it follows from these two arguments that prudence, identified by Morgenthau as the hallmark of realist foreign policy, is impossible without reflexivity.

Power politics, as understood by most realists, is both social and relational – it is not simply the ability to destroy, but the ability to affect political outcomes in a way that promotes the interests of the user of power. As Morgenthau defines it, "[p]ower may comprise anything that establishes and maintains the control of man over man."[28] What counts as power in any particular relationship, therefore, depends as much on the response of the object of a power relationship as on any specific capabilities of the user of power. "Its content and the manner of its use are determined by the political and cultural environment."[29] As such, the analysis of power politics requires sensitivity to particular political and cultural contexts. This refers both to those political and cultural norms that both ends of a power relationship share, and to those that they do not.

One might respond that this requirement can be met by the objective study of the political and cultural context of a given international interaction. But this objectivity is problematic in the case of realism as foreign policy analysis, because prescriptive foreign policy analysis presumes that the analyst is on one side of the interaction, or at minimum has some interest in the interaction. The realist analyst, in other words, as a prescriber of foreign policy is not a neutral observer of the interaction. To the extent that the realist's interest in the interaction is informed by a political morality, it becomes easy to read the situation

---

[27] Flyvbjerg 2001; Oren 2009.   [28] Morgenthau 1967, p. 9.
[29] Morgenthau 1967, p. 9.

through the lens of that morality. As Morgnethau notes, "[a]ll nations are tempted – and few have been able to resist the temptation for long – to clothe their own particular aspirations and actions in the moral purposes of the universe." But "realism refuses to identify the moral aspirations of a particular nation with the moral laws that govern the universe."[30] What is true of the nation is true of the analyst as well. There is an inherent (or, as Morgenthau puts it, "ineluctable") tension between the moral perspective from which the analyst sees the interaction, and the perspective from which those upon whom power is to be used are likely to see it. Reflexivity will not make this tension go away. But it will have the effect of reminding realists that the tension is there, that in order to understand the likely success of the application of political power in a particular situation they must look occasionally at the possibility that they are succumbing to the temptation to clothe their aspirations in a normative setting that they are projecting onto others.

The facile critic of realism might respond to this argument by pointing out that the argument is grounded in the concept of morality, and by arguing in turn that realism eschews morality as utopian, and focuses instead purely on power politics. But, as discussed in more detail in Chapter 8, power politics and morality cannot be so easily separated. "Political realism is aware of the moral significance of political action."[31] This statement, one of Morgenthau's six principles of political realism, indicates that classical realists did not in fact reject morality as a necessary part of foreign policy-making. In fact, they recognized that power without recognition of morality is as poor a guide to foreign policy as morality without recognition of power. "A man who was nothing but 'political man' would be a beast, for he would be completely lacking in moral restraints. A man who was nothing but 'moral man' would be a fool, for he would be completely lacking in prudence."[32] Or as Carr puts it, "we cannot ultimately find a resting place in pure realism; for realism, though logically overwhelming, does not provide us with the springs of action which are necessary even to the pursuit of thought." He then goes on to note that "a right of moral judgment" is one of the "essential ingredients of all effective political thinking."[33]

---

[30] Morgenthau 1967, p. 10.   [31] Morgenthau 1967, p. 9.
[32] Morgenthau 1967, p. 13.   [33] Carr 1964, p. 89.

Classical realism, then, argues that we must at the same time be clear in our own political morality, without which political action, and therefore foreign policy, is meaningless, and recognize that this morality is not universal. Not, of course, that we must accept all political moralities as equivalent, but that we must recognize that the moralities of both policy counterparts and mass publics elsewhere are genuinely held, and may be genuinely different from our own. This observation has three particularly relevant corollaries. The first is that foreign publics and elites are likely to see events in international politics, and our responses to these events, through the lens of their political morality. The second is that political moralities change. And the third is that our foreign policies can have a recursive effect on that change. Reflexivity helps the realist to deal with all three of these corollaries more effectively.

It helps to deal with the first corollary by making it more likely that realist scholars will reflect on how foreign policy is likely to look through the eyes of relevant others. Morgenthau was making precisely this point when he argued, in the context of the fifth of his six principles of political realism, that in our relations with other nations "we are able to do justice to all of them in a dual sense: We are able to judge other nations as we judge our own and, having judged them in this fashion, we are then capable of pursuing policies that respect the interests of other nations, while protecting and promoting those of our own."[34] We do judge both other nations and our own – without some grounding in a political morality, there is no point from which to analyze foreign policy in the first place. A reflexive realism, one that consciously attempts to apply the same standards of judgement to both ourselves and our antagonists, is one that is less likely to succumb to the utopian error that conflates the goals of foreign policy with the reality of the international political context in which that policy operates.

Not only do political moralities differ, but they change over time. A reflexive realism, one that occasionally applies the lens of realist analysis to itself, and that adopts the presumption of change across contexts that can be found in the works of the early realist authors, is well placed to recognize these changes before they become historical artifacts. It is certainly better placed to recognize such changes than a

---

[34] Morgenthau 1967, p. 11.

realism that operates on the methodological presumption of continuity across historical and geographical contexts. This is the point being made by Carr in the quotation above, about attacking realism with its own weapons. Reflexivity is needed to distinguish between situations where political moralities have not changed significantly, and those where change is simply not recognized by the analyst because of the analyst's own predisposition toward the status quo.

Not only do political moralities change, but such change is not necessarily independent of foreign policy. This final corollary of the observation that political morality matters but is not universal is related as well to the argument that realist power analysis demands reflexivity. To the extent that effective power politics depends as much on the response of the target as the capabilities of the user, power is mediated by political morality. The responses of the objects of power, in other words, depend in part on how they believe they should respond, normatively as well as strategically. That response can be affected by the original use of power in a variety of ways, both in the long term and in the short. It can do so, for example, by empowering certain interpreters of political morality at the expense of others, or by undermining the hold of an ideology on a population. It can also do so by breaking down the existing political order – as we see in failed states, once such an order is broken, it can be difficult, to say the least, to build up again. A reflexive realism, by asking how we might respond to an attempted use of power on us, will be better placed to foresee how an equivalent use of power by us might be seen by others.

The last of the arguments in favor of a reflexive realism, beyond the questions of power politics and morality already discussed, is that prudence in foreign policy requires it. This is the case for a variety of reasons. Prudence, or moderation, as Morgenthau sometimes phrases it,[35] requires, among other things, that we do not overestimate our national capabilities. This means most obviously not overestimating national power, but it also means not overestimating the appeal of our political morality to others (which is actually the same thing inasmuch as the appeal of our political morality to others is a source of power). This prudence calls for reflexivity for reasons that follow directly from the arguments in the paragraphs above.

[35] Morgenthau 1967, p. 11.

But it also requires that we not overestimate our analytical capabilities, as scholars as well as policy-makers. It requires that we not pretend to be more accurate in our predictions than the available evidence warrants – false confidence in our analytical abilities is nothing if not imprudent. It requires that we recognize the limits to our knowledge of and empathy for ways of thinking other than our own, and communicate these analytical limitations, along with the potential effects of these limitations on foreign policy prescriptions, to policy-makers.

Perhaps most fundamentally, it requires that we recognize our own cognitive limitations. It requires, in other words, that we accept reflexively that there may be political actors in other countries, responding to our foreign policy, who are cleverer than we are. This observation refers back to two key realist arguments, that political actors pursue power, and that power can take many forms, subject to historical context that is changeable. In a perfect game-theoretic world, we could model the strategic interactions generated by a given foreign policy decision, and deduce what our adversary's best option is. But in our imperfect world, there is always the possibility that our adversary will think of a better option in response to our policy than we had thought of. If power politics is key, then we must allow that other countries will be thinking about it as much as we are. The more a policy relies on specific responses by others, therefore, the more brittle it is likely to be. And brittle, in this context, is a reasonable antithesis to prudent. The more reflexive realists are in their thinking about foreign policy, the more likely they are to recognize their own cognitive limitations, and therefore to make moderate policy prescriptions that are robust enough to cope with the unpredictability of international politics, and the abilities of other users of power.

There are nevertheless limits to the use of reflexivity, much as there are limits to the use of the concept of power, for approaches to the study of international relations that are inductive, social, and contextual. Both constructivists and realists need to be aware that, in imposing an interpretation on empirical evidence, they are creating a reading of discourse or of normative structure that will not be universally shared, and that is subjective. But at the same time, they need to make such interpretations. Both constructivists and realists need to make arguments about intersubjective patterns of understanding based on readings of evidence that is itself objective (in the sense that the evidence is available to others, not in the sense that it is impartial). In other words, reflexivity for these approaches needs to be interpreted in a way that provides a check on analytic interpretation, not an obstacle to it. This is worth noting because there are approaches to the study of international relations that do see reflexivity as an obstacle. These include both behavioral approaches that claim objectivity, and those approaches, including deconstruction, that see any reading of evidence as inherently subjective, sufficiently so that such readings are suspect and are of value primarily for what they say about the interpreter.[36] Such approaches are incompatible with the logic of the social, and in fact reject the epistemology underlying the logic of the social.

How does one use reflexivity as a check without allowing it to be an obstacle? As noted in the introduction to this chapter, the answer is reasonableness. The line between a check and an obstacle cannot be found in fixed rules of research design, in elaborate methodological guidelines, or in the specifications of social theory. The line can only be found communicatively, in the process of researchers making the case for their interpretations to other students of international relations. As Kevin Dunn explains it, "[m]y goal as a researcher is to provide an argument about why my interpretation is valid, so that I can convince others that mine is one of the best interpretations out there."[37] This is in effect an "I know it when I see it" standard. But much as politics are contextual for approaches to the study of international relations that are grounded in a logic of the social, method for these approaches is contextual as well. To fetishize method is, for such approaches, to draw one's focus away from the study of politics.

Constructivism and theories of politics

A focus on reflexivity at the expense of argument is, of course, not the only manner of fetishizing method. And too much focus on reflexivity is no less problematic for constructivism than too little. In the context of approaches to the study of international relations that predominate in the academy in the United States, too little reflexivity is far more likely to be the case than too much.[38] This is most obviously the

---

[36] Waever 1996 and 1997. [37] Dunn 2006, p. 381.
[38] Smith 2002.

case with approaches that fetishize quantitative and formal methods, many of which appear to prioritize mathematical and statistical innovation over any discussion of politics *per se* (this is not to say that these methods are necessarily incompatible with a constructivist approach, but rather that *as practiced* in the discipline, particularly in the United States, they tend to be, because they are practiced without reflexivity).[39]

But much international relations scholarship is unreflexive in the realm of politics as well as in the realm of method. In the case of unreflexive realisms, this often happens at the expense of the internal consistency of the approach, because realism if done well, particularly as a theory of foreign policy, must be reflexive. In the case of many specific liberalisms, however, the absence of reflexivity is part and parcel of the approach. This is the case both with positive and normative approaches to liberalism.[40] In the case of positive liberalisms, the utilitarianism that underlies the approach is assumed rather than problematized. This pattern can be seen most clearly in neoclassical economics, in which the assumption that wealth equals utility is sufficiently fundamental that it goes unquestioned. In the field of international relations, neoliberal institutionalism displays this characteristic in its assumptions about the benefits of international cooperation.[41]

In the case of normative liberalisms, the absence of reflexivity is a core feature of the approach. Normative liberalism refers here to approaches to the study of international relations that begin with normative arguments about what the core features of international politics should be. The content of the normative argument is generally based on the concept of universal human rights. Such arguments may be purely normative (foreign policy should be designed to promote, for example, human rights), or may connect the normative and the empirical (arguing, for example, that a respect for human rights will end up creating a more peaceful world or serving the national

---

[39] In fact, practitioners of quantitative and formal methods criticize each other for fetishizing method at the expense of politics. See, for example, Green and Shapiro 1994 and Friedman 1995, respectively.

[40] On the distinction between positive and normative liberalism in international relations theory, see Reus-Smit 2001b.

[41] See, for example, Haas, Keohane, and Levy 1993, in which the authors allow that international institutions can prove counterproductive if they do not aid cooperation, but never question that cooperation itself is necessary.

interest).[42] But in either case the normative ideal is not approached reflexively – the point of a concept such as universal human rights is specifically that they are (in principle, at least) universal, not contextual. Liberalisms in general tend to be based on transhistorical ideals, whether those ideals are empirical (people are utility maximizers) or normative (individual rights should be respected).

This observation is notable in this context because constructivism as practiced, particularly in the United States, is often of a liberal bent, and in particular of a normative liberal bent. Constructivist work, particularly of the thin or neoclassical variety, has often focused on norms such as human rights and cooperation, and often in a way that accepts these normative stances unproblematically, as transhistorical givens.[43] But human rights or cooperation accepted as a universal goal of politics sits awkwardly with the constructivist assumption that norms are historically contextual.

This is not to suggest that constructivism and liberalism are incompatible (although constructivism and some positive liberalisms may be epistemologically incompatible[44]). Nor is it a critique of liberalism. Rather, it is to note that the two approaches are in important ways orthogonal to each other. Constructivism is empirical social theory, while normative liberalism is political theory. Normative theory, or idealism if one prefers to call it that,[45] informs decisions by researchers about what to research, and decisions by both policy-makers and publics about what the goals of policy should be. Constructivism looks to existent discourses and norms. Those discourses and norms may be liberal, they may not be. A constructivist approach is certainly an appropriate one to use to ask whether they are or not, and to ask how liberal norms can be disseminated, how the use of liberal discourses can be expanded. Such an approach can also be used in conjunction with normative commitments other than liberalism. The key to doing so and still using constructivist method effectively is reflexivity, the recognition that the link between motive and norm that looks benign

---

[42] See, for example, Schulz 2001.   [43] Barkin 2003a.

[44] Steele 2007.

[45] Idealism seems to be the preferred term of those who argue that normative theory is not what we should be focusing on in international relations theory. See, for example, Legro and Moravcsik 1999 and Wendt 1999. Morgenthau 1946 speaks of liberalism specifically rather than idealism generally, and Carr 1964 speaks of utopianism rather than idealism.

to the researcher or policy-maker may look less benign to those not currently part of the intersubjective understanding underlying the norm. It is this reflexive moment that is sometimes missing in liberal constructivist analyses.

It is worth noting in this context that what was said in the previous paragraph about the relationship among constructivism, normative liberalism, and reflexivity applies equally to the relationship among realism, normative liberalism, and reflexivity. Classical realism and predictive liberalism, that subset of liberal approaches to the study of international relations that predict behavior based on assumptions of rational utility-maximizing behavior, are incompatible. But the same is not true of realism and normative liberalisms. Classical realism demands some normative content to the national interest, and that content can well be liberal. In fact, one can argue that for some of the key classical realists it was.[46] Realism in this sense does not eschew normative commitments, but asks us to recognize that because those commitments are not universally accepted, they will be opposed by others. This opposition in turn effectively limits what can be accomplished through national means in pursuing those commitments.

The upshot is that since both constructivist and realist logics are social and contextual, and since both recognize that politics requires a public interest but neither brings with it particular normative commitments, both approaches share a similar relationship with normative theories of international politics. One can indeed have a normatively liberal constructivism;[47] but then, one can also have a liberal realism.[48] But one can only do so successfully, in either case, with a reflexivity that allows one to see one's normative commitment from the perspective of others, a reflexivity that is reasonable rather than dogmatic.

Methodology and the social

The third constraint discussed in this chapter on approaches to the study of international relations that combine a logic of the social

---

[46] Morgenthau's commitment to peace, which shares equal billing in the title of his best-known book with power (Morgenthau 1948), is (arguably) a liberal commitment.

[47] Steele 2007 argues against a liberal constructivism, but his argument focuses on positive liberal international relations theory, not normative liberal international relations theory.

[48] But then, one could just as well have both a constructivist and a realist socialism, or any other normative political -ism.

with contextual interpretation is on methodology. This constraint is actually a relatively loose one. Any method that can address questions of intersubjective understandings can be used to study the social construction of international politics. While constructivism is generally associated with interpretive methodology,[49] this association should not be taken to limit the approach only to narrative methods (method being understood here as specific information-gathering and processing techniques, as opposed to the more general way of thinking about information implied by the term methodology).[50]

The only exceptions, the only methodologies that are inappropriate to a constructivist approach, are those that are self-consciously opposed to the concept of intersubjectivity. And this is in fact quite rare. Quantitative methodology, for example, is neutral on the concept. If data on intersubjectivity (discourse use, poll data, etc.) can be assembled, they can be analyzed quantitatively.[51] Whether or not such analysis is useful in describing a pattern of intersubjectivity is no doubt open to interpretation in particular cases. But there is no *a priori* reason that it should necessarily not be useful. To use another example, some recent work suggests new game-theoretical techniques that are specifically designed to highlight the intersubjective.[52]

The constraints on approaches to the study of international politics that are grounded in a logic of the social, then, are primarily ontological and epistemological, and only secondarily methodological. The constraints are to be found more in the reading of the findings than in the method used. While constructivism is interpretive in its methodology, it can be quite eclectic in its method. By the same token realism, to the extent that it is grounded in a logic of the social, must also be methodologically interpretive, whatever its method.

---

[49] Klotz and Lynch 2007.
[50] For an example of an experimental methodology used in conjunction with constructivist social theory, see Hoffmann 2005.
[51] See, for example, Chwieroth 2007.
[52] For example Arfi 2005; Hoffmann 2005.

7 | Agency

The past three chapters have been devoted to discussing the inherently social aspects of both constructivism and realism. Yet at the same time there has been some discussion of the limits of focusing purely on the social. Chapter 4 noted that a focus only on a "logic of appropriateness" allows no more scope for change in patterns of international politics than does Waltz's transhistorical approach. And I have claimed in a number of places in previous chapters that the co-constitution of social structure and agents is a core concept of constructivism. Why the focus on the structure end of the agent–structure dialectic, and the relative absence of discussion of the role of agency?

Because you can theorize structure. But you can't theorize agency.

Or, to be more precise, within the context of the constructivist approach to international relations theory, one cannot reasonably make the sort of general statements about agents that one can about social structures. In other words, you can't theorize agency as agency is understood in constructivist logic. By general statements I do not refer to transhistorical ones, such as the neorealist claim that states in anarchy will always threaten each other. Rather, I refer to generalizations grounded in specific historical contexts – for example, the generalization that the norm of diplomatic immunity is widely subjectified in contemporary international politics, and therefore will continue to be respected most of the time in the near future.[1] Constructivist logic does not allow for even this limited sort of generalization about agency. Note that I am actually making a narrow claim here, that one cannot theorize about the actions and discourses of specific agents, as agents are understood in the context of the constructivist understanding of the agent–structure dialectic. There are several other understandings of agency that can be theorized, as will be noted below, and

[1] See, for example, Kier and Mercer 1996, p. 80.

even within the context of constructivism one can certainly debate what constitutes agency.

Several related questions stem from the argument that constructivists can't theorize agency. Where does human agency come from? How do other approaches to the study of international relations deal with the question of agency? If constructivists can't theorize agency, but agency provides the node in the agent–structure dialectic that allows for change, how can constructivism deal with change? This chapter addresses (although it does not necessarily answer) these questions.

It also looks at the role of agency in realist theory, and the extent to which the relationship between theory and agency is similar in classical realism and constructivism. I argue that the attempt by some contemporary realists to write agency out of realist theory undermines the core argument of realism. This provides a link to Chapter 8, on the limits of realism (as the arguments about agency and change provide a link to Chapter 9, on the limits of constructivism). But before addressing any of these questions and issues, a prior step is to lay out the logic supporting the core argument of this chapter, that there are severe limits on the extent to which one can generalize about agency from within the constructivist approach.

Theorizing agency

Alex Wendt defines agents in the context of social theory as "purposeful actors whose actions help reproduce or transform the society in which they live."[2] In other words, he defines them as people,[3] and as the component units of social structure. But not people as automatons, as cogs in a structure; rather, people who act purposefully, who are able to have an impact in the reproduction or transformation of the structures within which they find themselves. One can understand this definition broadly, to include people whose actions are determined by others, by the social structure itself, by the biological structures of their brains that cause them automatically, without thinking, to

[2] Wendt 1987, p. 338.
[3] Wendt 1999 also applies the term "actor" to corporate agents, organizations that behave in a purposive way. Whether or not one is sympathetic to the concept of corporate agency does not affect the status of the argument presented below. For an argument against the assumption of corporate agency in international relations theory, see Wight 2006.

behave in a certain way. Or one can understand this definition more narrowly, to focus on behaviors that individuals purposively choose to undertake, behaviors that are affected by but not determined by the structures, social or biological, within which actors find themselves. I take the latter route.

Defining agency narrowly makes sense in this context, because without this narrow definition there is no mechanism for change in an agent–structure dialectic. Behavior that is determined by structure, be that structure social or biological, can be expected to be consistent as long as the structure remains the same. The only mechanism for change without agency in the narrow, active sense is change in the external environment that affects structures. But given the focus in constructivist logic on social structure rather than material environment, relying on forces outside of the intersubjective as the primary source of change is problematic.[4] Understanding agency as part of the intersubjective, as making decisions that change people's understandings of the world in which they live, is a much more viable mechanism for change in this context.

Given this narrower definition, one can't theorize agency, because to theorize agency is to deny agency. One can theorize space for agency, places within social structures or times that are most conducive to manipulation by political actors to maximum effect. For example, one could argue with respect to places within social structures that effective agency is easier for those individuals with positions of authority in recognized and accepted social structures than it is for individuals without such positions (note that this should not be taken to imply that it is necessarily easy for those with such institutional backing, or impossible for those without).[5] One could argue with respect to times that the periods immediately after systemic wars tend to be times in which the norm structure of international politics is in flux, and as such times at which agency on the part of leaders of the winning coalition in the war is most likely to yield major changes in said norm structure.[6] One can also theorize factors that enable agency. For

---

[4] Ruggie 1983 argues that change can be generated from within the structure by increases in the density of social interactions. But this allows only a fairly narrow scope for change, and in any case begs the question of where the increased density came from.

[5] See, for example, the discussion of norm entrepreneurs in Finnemore and Sikkink 1998.

[6] Barkin and Cronin 1994.

example, one can argue that greater education empowers people to act more effectively with respect to bureaucratized social institutions, or that certain internal political structures grant the national executive more leeway in foreign policy-making than others.[7]

Similarly, one can theorize constraints on agency, of a variety of kinds. These constraints can be external (constraints imposed by social structures within which agents find themselves) or internal (psychological or cognitive limitations on what agents can do, or think or feel that they can do).[8] The constraints can involve the interaction of the external and internal, such as cognitive biases toward in-group cohesion and intergroup conflict.[9] Constraints can be absolute (agents cannot do x from within a certain structure), partial (agents will find it more difficult to do x from within one structure than another), or probabilistic (agents have a certain specific likelihood of doing x in a particular situation).

Ultimately, however, theorizing of this sort, whether it is about space for agency or constraints on agency, is about structure. To say that agency is affected in a certain way by a certain social structure, or a certain pattern of change in social structure, or by a given understanding of human nature or human psychology and cognition, is to place a constraint on individual agency, narrowly understood. Even theorizing enabling conditions for agency is to theorize constraints, inasmuch as these conditions are the absence of theorized constraints. And theorizing enabling conditions in any case is not the same as theorizing the content of agency, predicting what agents will do. To predict what an agent will do is in effect denying that agent agency – it is to say that the agent lacks either the will or the ability (or both) to act in a manner different from that dictated by his or her constraints, be those constraints external (social structure) or internal (psychological or biological).

Theorizing agency in the context of a constructivist approach to the study of international relations is then in essence impossible by definition. Agency narrowly understood means the potential for unpredictability, for unpatterned behavior. Theories of agency are attempts to find patterns in behavior. Therefore it is tautological that agency cannot be theorized.

---

[7] Waltz 1967.
[8] See Waltz 1979 and Jervis 1976, respectively, for examples.
[9] For example Mercer 1995.

Three clear limits on this claim should be noted at this point. The first is that I am referring in my argument to theorizing the content of agency, not the potential for agency. To say that a given situation has a potential for agency (such as in the example above about the aftermath of great power wars), that it is likely to generate new thinking on the part of an actor, is to comment on changing structural conditions while still leaving the actor scope for agency, scope to act in ways that are not predetermined. To say that the actor will do a specific thing in response to those changing conditions is to deny that actor agency.

The second limit is to be found in the specific way in which I am using the term "theory." I am using it to mean predictive theory, rather than explanatory or prescriptive theory. In other words, the claim is that one cannot from a constructivist perspective make general arguments about what agents will do. I do not mean to claim that one cannot reasonably develop explanatory theories about particular agents or acts of agency.[10] The specific use of the term "theory" here is a rhetorical tool, intended to emphasize the point. It should not be taken as an argument that predictive theory in any way takes primacy over explanatory or descriptive theory.[11] This also does not mean that constructivists should not predict, but these predictions must be contingent on agency.

The third limit on the claim that one cannot theorize agency has already been noted – the claim is made in the context of constructivist logic specifically, and empirically driven approaches to the study of international relations more broadly. It does not apply to normative theory. One can certainly theorize what agents *should* do, without assuming that they necessarily *will* do it, without in any way denying them their agency. In fact, for an actor to access a normative argument and choose to act accordingly reaffirms rather than denies her or his agency. Any reasoned action by an agent (as opposed to reactive or habitual action) most likely draws on normative theory, making such theory an integral part of human agency.[12] But, as argued in various places in this book, constructivism is not normative theory.

[10] For example Finnemore 1996a.
[11] For an example of an argument that only predictive theory (and, more specifically, inferential theory) is legitimate social science, see King, Keohane, and Verba 1994.
[12] This is the point that both Carr 1964 and Morgenthau 1948 are making when they talk about political morality, as discussed both in the previous chapter and the next one.

But do not other approaches to the study of international relations attempt to theorize agency? Ultimately, no, they do not, in the sense that agency is being used here. Other approaches to the study of international relations theorize space for agency or constraints on agency; they use agency to explain specific historical outcomes, or they make normative arguments about agency. When using the terminology of agent and agency, they use it with a different meaning than the one used here, and they therefore are not theorizing agency directly as I define the term here. Note that I am not making the claim that these other uses of the term are wrong, or inaccurate, or inappropriate. But they are distinct from the meaning of the term in the context of the constructivist agent–structure dialectic. Four examples of such approaches serve to illustrate this point: liberal theory, rational choice theory, critical theory, and political psychology and cognition.

Liberalism has generated a broad variety of theoretical approaches to the study of international relations. Some of these are clearly normative theory, and deal with agency in a clearly normative way. For example, an argument that our national foreign policy should promote universal human rights as a matter of principle is clearly normative – it is an argument about what we (or our national representatives) should do as agents, intended to make it more likely that we do it, but not predicting that we necessarily will. This category of liberal theory is orthogonal to the argument being made here. Other branches of liberal theory in the study of international relations, however, are predictive rather than normative.

One example of such a branch is democratic peace theory. This theory argues that democracies do not make war on each other. Various strands of the democratic peace argument come at it from very different directions – some make statistical arguments showing that democracies historically have not fought, and others make process-oriented arguments about why the domestic political processes of democratic states restrain them from going to war against other democracies.[13] While these two strands make very different sorts of arguments, the arguments have in common that they are in a fundamental way structural. Neither leaves room for agency, as defined here. Both arguments are also transhistorical, in that they imply that any time two

---

[13] For the former, see Russett and Oneal 2001 and Chan 1997. For the latter see Owen 1994 and Bueno de Mesquita *et al.* 1999.

polities have a certain formal constitutional structure, they will not make war on each other. There is no historical contingency here, no room for different social contexts or intersubjective understandings of political process. In this sense, both strands are asocial, meaning that democratic peace theory does not fit into the agency–social structure dialectic at all.[14]

But beyond this absence of the social, democratic peace theory is premised on the assumption that people as individuals either will not act outside of structurally determined scripts, or that such actions will not affect outcomes in international politics. The statistical strand is based on the premise that people will act in the future in the same way that they have acted in the past.[15] Without this premise, the conclusions of this strand are of purely historical interest, without any predictive or policy relevance. And the domestic process strand is based on the assumption that people will react to a given political structure in a given way. It is based on the assumption that the weight of preference in democratic polities will be for peaceful relations with other democracies, based on certain specific assumptions about human nature, and that either there will be no significant dissent, or that this dissent will not be sufficient to change policy.[16] In other words, that individual agency (actors doing things in ways that are not directly determined by structure) will be insufficient to meaningfully affect structurally determined outcomes (structure in this context being constitutional rather than social structure more broadly).

Rational choice theory does not assume that people will continue to behave according to a set historical pattern, or that they will be fully constrained by political structures. It does, however, deal with agency in a different way, by assuming that people behave according to a set script, this script being defined by the concept of instrumental rationality. There is in fact space in rational choice theory for agency, prior to the script that defines human behavior. It is to be found in

---

[14] See Steele 2007 for a more fully fleshed-out version of this argument, that concludes that democratic peace theory is incompatible with constructivism.

[15] See, for example, Russett 1993.

[16] In the case of rational choice arguments to this effect (for example Bueno de Mesquita *et al.* 1999) there is no space for agency for reasons that will be discussed in the next paragraph, on rational choice theory. In the case of belief-based arguments (for example Owen 1994), there is an implicit assumption that once democratic processes and liberal norms are combined in a polity, they will continue to predominate.

preferences, which are exogenous to the assumptions of this approach (although the more economistic approaches to rational choice theory often assume that money can be used as a fungible indicator for preferences, denying agency to individuals even there). But those approaches to rational choice theory that allow for individual agency in preferences have nothing to say about those preferences – agency remains exogenous to the theory.[17] Some approaches to rational choice theory induce preferences from observed behavior, thereby assuming *a priori* that people never think in a way that departs from the instrumental rationality script.[18] Individuals, on this approach, can display agency in their preferences, but by definition cannot do so in the way that they process information and make decisions. Other approaches allow that individuals can act in ways not predicted by the theory. But such behaviors are often referred to as "pathological."[19] Agency, on this view, is pathological, a sign of cognitive failure.

Rational choice theory does itself speak of agency, the most prominent current example being principal–agent models.[20] But the concept of agency as used in principal–agent models is completely different from the concept of agent that constructivists understand to be in a dialectical relationship with structure. Agents in rational choice theory are those who act on behalf of someone else (as in "real estate agent"), rather than someone who acts purposefully to reproduce or transform their society.[21] The use of the same word masks reference to concepts that are in a way opposites of each other. The agent of principal–agent theory, who is expected to act in a predictable way in response to given incentives, is not an agent in the constructivist sense.

Critical theory does not attempt to script human behavior in the way that both rational choice theory and predictive liberal theory do. It does not, in this sense, try to deny human agency by predicting

---

[17] Some rational choice arguments, for example, assume that actors occupy a particular place on an ideological spectrum, and that this place defines their interests, but do not address the question of how they got to that place on the spectrum. See, for example, Milner 1997.

[18] For example Bueno de Mesquita 1981 and 1985.

[19] See, for example, Fearon 1995. See also Green and Shapiro 1994.

[20] See, for example, Nielson and Tierney 2003 and Pollack 1997.

[21] These two usages follow from two distinct definitions of the word "agent," as a "person who acts for another" and as a "person who or thing which produces an effect," respectively. Oxford University Press 2002, p. 41.

that structure is determinative. Like liberal theory, critical theory has generated a wide variety of specific approaches to the study of international relations, and thus generalizing too much about the relationship between critical theory and agency is problematic. As is the case with liberal theory, some critical theory deals with agency normatively rather than empirically, focusing on what people should do rather than predicting what they will do.[22] Similarly, some critical theory focuses on explaining past agency, rather than attempting to predict future agency.[23]

Where critical theory in general differs most clearly both from liberal theory and from rational choice theory with respect to its treatment of agency in international relations is in the absence from any major strand of critical theory of an equivalent to assumptions of patterned or instrumentally rational behavior, that attempts to deny agency by subsuming it to a determinative account of human behavior. Critical theorists tend to focus on the social and discursive power structures that constrain agency, with the goal of emancipation from those structures. While various critical theorists may well have somewhat different meanings in mind for the concept of emancipation, it is generally used as an enabling condition rather than a constraining one, a condition that allows a broader scope for individual agency rather than one that attempts to define a content for agency. Critical theory on the whole, therefore, does not attempt to theorize agency in the way that this phrase is being used here, but rather focuses on enabling it.

Finally, theories of political psychology and political cognition tend not to speak of agency as such. When they do, they use it to make room for the effects of individuals, rather than social structures, on international politics. But this is done in the context of psychological patterns of behavior that mediate between social structure and outcome.[24] Ultimately then, though they speak of agents, these approaches are using the term differently from its meaning in the context of the constructivist agent–structure dialectic. They are in effect theorizing structure. Structure at a biological/physiological, rather than social, level, but structure nonetheless, rather than agency in the constructivist sense.

---

[22] For example Murphy 2001.   [23] For example Murphy 1994.
[24] See, for example, Shannon 2000.

Agency, constructivism, and human nature

These theories of political psychology and cognition are in essence attempts to deal scientifically and, often, experimentally with the question of human nature. Most approaches to the study of international relations deal with human nature by assumption rather than by experiment, and constructivists by and large fall into this latter group.[25] As noted in Chapter 3, all such approaches require some theory about human nature, whether assumed or induced, as a starting point. A key difference between defensive and offensive realism, two strands of contemporary neorealism, for example, is that the former assumes that the stronger motivating factor in human nature is fear, the latter that it is greed.[26] Rational choice theory begins with the assumption that it is human nature to be instrumentally rational.[27]

Liberal international relations theory more broadly, one could argue, is generally based on some variant of the assumption that human nature is perfectible. The variation is in what perfectibility is assumed to be. In rationalist variants, the assumption is that we can study international relations as if it were human nature to be perfectly rational (whether rationality is taken to mean instrumental rationality or reasoned discourse). Both neoliberal institutionalist and democratic peace theories assume that if we get the institutions right (international institutions for the former, domestic political institutions for the latter), then international relations will become cooperative. In the former case, international cooperation is the default condition, needing only international institutions that effectively ameliorate the market failures that prevent cooperation.[28] In the latter case, it is imperfect domestic political structures that lead to war – get those structures right, and the problem of war goes away.[29]

Constructivists generally begin with very different assumptions about human nature. A necessary assumption about human nature underlying constructivist logic is that it is social, that humans participate in social institutions, hold intersubjective understandings,

---

[25] But see Mercer 1995 for an exception.
[26] Rose 1998; Mearsheimer 2001.
[27] Or, in many instances, with the assumption that we can reasonably study human behavior as if this were true. See, for example, Scott 2000.
[28] Martin and Simmons 1998.
[29] Russett and Oneal 2001.

because it is in their nature to do so. To posit as a starting point of a discussion of an approach to social science that people's identities, interests, ideas, and discourses are constructed from the social milieu in which they find themselves is to assume that they are inherently social beings. This follows clearly from the discussion of the logic of the social in Chapters 4–6, above. Of course, this logic of the social applies to realist as well as to constructivist logic, implying that realism shares with constructivism the assumption that sociality is an inherent part of human nature. More on this below.[30]

Jennifer Sterling-Folker argues that the assumption of sociability in the view of human nature underlying constructivism is at minimum in tension with, and at maximum ultimately incompatible with, the assumption of perfectibility underlying the predominant liberal approaches to the study of international relations. She takes to task liberal constructivists, particularly Alex Wendt, for positing a "systematic space beyond existing national identities [that] can apparently be filled with a more rational discourse based on collective problems as they exist 'out there' rather than as they exist 'in here' where our identities actually originate."[31] She argues that in adopting such functionalist arguments, based on the idea that social institutions are perfectible, "the most basic tenets of constructivism are violated."[32]

The sociability of constructivist human nature, Sterling-Folker argues, has implications for our view of human political behavior. It "means that we form groups – implying division, competition, and structural concerns with relative power."[33] These implications are part and parcel of the assumption of sociability, the assumption that individuals define themselves in reference to the groups within which they find themselves. Sociability therefore accounts, following this logic, for a dialectic of in-group and out-group social interaction – "we are inevitably and simultaneously capable of unity-universalism and division-particularism. These tendencies cannot be separated analytically or philosophically."[34] Group dynamics, as a result, cannot be reduced to functional needs.[35] The dialectical nature of the

---

[30] On human nature, logics of the social, and how these concepts interrelate in the context of realism, constructivism, and liberalism, see Sterling-Folker 2000, 2004, and 2006a.

[31] Sterling-Folker 2000, p. 114.   [32] Sterling-Folker 2000, p. 108.

[33] Sterling-Folker 2004, p. 342.   [34] Sterling-Folker 2004, p. 342.

[35] Shannon 2000.

relationship between universalism and particularism belies any single hierarchy of functional needs, and therefore does not allow for the perfectibility of any set of political institutions. This argument applies to any approach to the study of international relations governed by a logic of the social. In other words, as Sterling-Folker notes, it applies as much to realism as it does to constructivism.[36]

Agency, co-constitution, and change

The argument to this point is that constructivism is about co-constitution of agency and structure, that structure is social and that this sociability is an artifact of human nature, that the agency part of this dialectic is crucial for understanding change in international politics, but that we can't theorize that agency. How do we talk about co-constitution with the structural end of the dialectic not only theorized but grounded in human nature, without theorizing the agency end of the dialectic?

We do so by identifying the role of agency historically, by identifying the ways in which agency has been and can be used to both reinforce and change structure, by noting the ways in which particular social structures need agency to be continually recreated, and perhaps by speculating on the ways in which agents might react to a given structure. But whereas social structure can be thought of as epistemologically inertial (i.e. that a reasonable assumption of how a social structure will look tomorrow, barring changed conditions or agency, is the way it looks today), agency is the opposite. Agency is the unexpected.

This unexpectedness defines one of the limits of empirical approaches to the study of international relations that are grounded in a logic of the social. Co-constitution allows us to look at ways in which social structures are being recreated and changed, and it allows us to identify how new structures came into being historically. But it cannot tell us how agents will behave, what agents will say, with respect to social structures in the future. Constructivist logic thus allows us to predict structure into the (near) future in a contingent way, but does not allow us to predict agency even to this extent.

An interesting aside at this point is that, because of this inability to predict agency, constructivism as an approach to the study

---

[36] Sterling-Folker 2004.

of international relations cannot deal at all with psychopaths, with those individuals who are not tethered by social structures in ways we can understand. It cannot deal, in other words, with people whose interaction with social structures is purely subjective rather than intersubjective. If these individuals manage to create new social realities, new intersubjectivities, then these new social structures can be understood in constructivist terms. But the subjective logic that leads the individual to generate these institutions in the first place remains opaque to any approach to the study of international relations grounded in a logic of the social. Constructivism can help us to understand, for example, the social milieu in which Hitler decided to devote such great effort to genocide, and the discursive mechanisms by which he was able to institutionalize his decision, but the decision itself necessarily remains opaque to an approach grounded in the social.[37]

Agency is the mechanism for change in constructivism, but constructivism cannot theorize agency. Constructivism as an approach is therefore limited in the extent to which it can theorize change in international relations. By looking at the co-constitution of agents and structures, constructivists can explain past changes, and can extrapolate predictions of change in particular institutions, but can say little about general patterns of change in the institutional patterns of international politics. This latter observation should not be surprising, given that theorizing about general patterns of change would in effect be making transhistorical claims. But it is worth noting more broadly that constructivists cannot extrapolate within the construct of their epistemology in the same way as can scholars working within traditions that do not emphasize co-constitution and historical contingency.

Does this mean that constructivism itself, despite its claims of distinctiveness from transhistorical approaches that cannot address change in the institutional structure of international relations, has little to say about change? No. It just means that constructivist logic has certain limits to its ability to predict change, limits that are different from those of approaches grounded in different epistemologies.

---

[37] An approach grounded in the social can tell us quite a bit about conditions of possibility created by his particular social context, but those conditions neither determined that genocide would happen, nor explain why it was Hitler specifically who led it.

Constructivists can, however, say a variety of other things about change in international politics. Most clearly, they can identify the mechanisms of change, in ways that approaches to the study of international relations that look to transhistorical arguments cannot. The ability to identify the mechanisms of change in turn allows constructivists to do three things. The first, already noted, is explaining historical change in the international system. The second is identifying social structures in which change is likely, because patterns of the reconstitution of those structures by agents are either weakening or changing. Not necessarily predicting what change will happen, but rather simply that change is likely to happen. And the third is prescribing rather than predicting agency. Constructivist analysis of social structures can yield useful tactical advice for those agents who wish to change particular social structures. Constructivist theory cannot tell agents what they should want to change – that is a task for normative, rather than empirical, theory. But it can provide useful analysis about how to go about changing social structures, once agents have decided to do so.[38]

This constraint on what can be said about agency from within a constructivist epistemology leaves constructivist practitioners navigating a fairly thin road between ignoring agency and overdetermining agency. An example of the perils of this road can be found in the concept of "norm cascades," a concept that has found some purchase among many constructivists as a model of norm change, of how norms spread.[39] Martha Finnemore and Kathryn Sikkink argue that norm cascades are the middle stage in a three-stage process of norm diffusion, between norm emergence and internationalization. This middle stage is marked by the transition from altruistic, committed norm entrepreneurs as carriers of the norm in its initial phase, to formal institutions, such as states, acting for legitimacy and reputation as they see the norm cascading into general acceptance. The final stage, internalization, is marked by the legalization and bureaucratization of the norm, and a transition from strategically motivated behavior to appropriate behavior.

[38] And constructivists can then, of course, analyze the intersubjective understandings that played a part in constituting the agent in the first place, and the role of agency in generating those understandings, and so forth in infinite regression.

[39] Finnemore and Sikkink 1998.

To argue that norms cascade in this fashion, through this sequence of actors, in a particular case, or in a variety of particular cases, is entirely reasonable (given supporting evidence, of course). To suggest that a cascade can be a useful metaphor for understanding the spread of norms is also reasonable, subject to the understanding that the metaphor may not always be appropriate, and to the caveat that such a metaphor can become tautological if it is stretched too far, and thereby become of little analytical use (if one defines any process of a norm catching on in a wider public as a cascade, then any time a norm becomes politically salient it will by definition have cascaded). But to derive from the concept of norm cascades a model of the diffusion of norms that applies generally is to create a transhistorical theory of agency.[40] And to place too much emphasis on the cascade model risks reading events exclusively through the lens of the model. This in turn is problematic in that it can undermine reflexivity, as discussed in the previous chapter.

A similar argument can be made for a concept like "norm entrepreneurs."[41] Clearly, the idea that norm entrepreneurs can have a major impact on international politics is entirely compatible with constructivist logic. There is room for debate about how much impact norm entrepreneurs have historically tended to have – the idea of norm entrepreneurs implies that individuals consciously decide to try to change normative structures, whereas some scholars might argue that norm change primarily happens through accretion, and through unintended effects.[42] This debate, however, is about the effects of norm entrepreneurs, not about the entrepreneurs themselves. Little can be said about the entrepreneurs themselves from within a constructivist perspective, other than to say that they do not follow a clear pattern, because if they did they would not be effective entrepreneurs. An analogy can be found in the literature on business entrepreneurs. There is a large literature out there on how to get ahead as a business entrepreneur. But the utility of this literature from the perspective of the

---

[40] Whether or not this is what Finnemore and Sikkink intend to do is not clear – their language (for example, "[n]orm influence may be understood as a three-stage process") can be understood to propose either a model or a metaphor. Finnemore and Sikkink 1998, p. 895.

[41] Finnemore and Sikkink 1998.

[42] Compare, for example, the idea of norm entrepreneurs with the focus on habit in Hopf 2002.

aspiring entrepreneur is limited – if a book gave accurate instructions about how to be relatively successful as an entrepreneur, and it came to be read by a majority of aspiring entrepreneurs, then it could no longer be accurate, because the majority cannot all be relatively successful at the same time. The book would then have succeeded in changing over time what it takes to be a relatively successful entrepreneur, rather than successfully identifying what it takes.

E. H. Carr sums up this effect with respect to international relations at the beginning of *The Twenty Years' Crisis*, suggesting that the effect applies to classical realist thought as well as constructivist.

The investigator is inspired by the desire to cure some ill of the body politic. Among the causes of the trouble, he diagnoses the fact that human beings normally react to certain conditions in a certain way. But this is not a fact comparable with the fact that human bodies react in a certain way to certain drugs. It is a fact which may be changed by the desire to change it; and this desire, already present in the mind of the investigator, may be extended, as the result of his investigation, to a sufficient number of other human beings to make it effective.[43]

Theorizing agency in these sorts of ways is a particular problem for those who combine constructivist and liberal approaches to the study of international relations. Liberal constructivists generally draw on the normative rather than rationalist strands of liberal theory (not surprisingly, given the methodological and ontological tensions between constructivist logic and methodological individualism). Constructivist methods are entirely compatible with liberal normative commitments. But there is a danger on the part of the researcher in transposing those commitments from a belief that they represent norms that should be universalized, to a belief that they represent norms that can be universalized. The common belief underlying much liberal IR theory that human nature is ultimately perfectible, and that the creation of appropriate social institutions will enable that perfectibility, is incompatible with constructivist logic both because it is in effect theorizing agency, and because it is non-reflexive.

Constructivists therefore need to allow for agency as the source of change, but need as well to recognize that agency is inherently unpredictable. The core concept of this approach, as noted above, is grounded in the logic of the social and in a focus on historical

---

[43] Carr 1964, p. 4.

contingency. Previous chapters have argued that this logic and focus is one that constructivism shares with classical realism. This in turn suggests that everything that has been said to this point about agency and constructivism applies as well to classical realism's relationship with agency. It suggests that realists should not be in the business of either denying a role for agency in international politics by arguing that structures, of whatever sort, are determinative, or of theorizing agency. For classical realism, a prudent foreign policy is one that recognizes, and allows for, the unpredictability of agency.[44]

So what?

Discussion of the role of agency in international relations implies a discussion of human nature. All approaches to the study of international relations contain assumptions, whether implicit or explicit, about human nature. The assumption underlying constructivism is that human nature is social. As Sterling-Folker argues, this sociality contains within it the seeds of both cooperation and conflict, both in-group and out-group behaviors. The assumption of sociality therefore suggests that we can expect international politics to display patterns both of cooperation and of conflict, and that neither pattern can in principle be ontologically privileged over the other.

Having said this, the idea of co-constitution that is a core element of constructivist thinking implies that human nature is agentive as well as social. In other words, human identity, the way in which we understand and define ourselves, is drawn from our social context, but at the same time we are able to act in response to this context in ways that are purposive as well as simply reactive. The content of this agency cannot, in the context of constructivism, in the general case be predicted – if it could, it would not be agency, it would simply be reactive behavior. A constructivist approach to the agency end of the agent–structure dialectic is therefore limited in what it can do. It can look at the effects of social structure on the self-understandings of agency, it can look at structural constraints on agency, it can look at the social mechanisms through which agency might express itself in particular historical contexts, and it can address questions of the importance of particular agents in generating change in patterns of

[44] Ashley 1984.

international politics. But it cannot theorize agency in the general case.

The same argument holds true for any approach to the study of international relations premised on a logic of the social, including realism. Like constructivism, realism implicitly assumes a human nature that is social, and that includes both in-group and out-group dynamics. Without this assumption, the idea of a national interest simply does not make sense. Specific realists may have explicitly added various additional (and, cumulatively, mutually contradictory) assumptions about human nature to this. However, realism more broadly can make sense without the added assumptions, but cannot make sense without the basic assumption of human sociability. If combined with an acceptance that individuals can act agentively, and that we cannot theorize this agency effectively, this logic of the social places clear limits on what can be predicted with realist theory. The seminal realist theorists of the middle of the twentieth century recognized these limits, which provide the source of their injunctions that we show prudence, and even some humility, in the conduct of foreign policy. The resultant limits on what can reasonably be done in the context of realist logic are the focus of the next chapter.

8 | The limits of realism

What limits are placed on realist theory by the logic of the social that inheres in classical realism's basic assumptions about international politics? When combined with the relationship between realism and reflexivity discussed in Chapter 6, this logic constrains realism from confidently predicting outcomes. This proposition may at first seem absurd, given the claims of several strands of contemporary realism specifically to be scientifically predictive. But the core argument in this chapter is that these strands not only fail to fulfill claims of some contemporary realist theorists to be both predictive and prescriptive, but that too much focus on being predictive, on being scientific, also undermines the core insight of classical realism.[1]

This core insight, as phrased by Hans Morgenthau, is that we must see the world as it is, rather than as we want it to be. "Political realism believes that politics, like society in general, is governed by objective laws."[2] This observation seems, at first glance, to support an argument that realism is about scientific prediction. But embedded in this core insight is the claim that the realist world, the world as it is, is not that neatly predictable. "The first lesson the student of international politics must learn and never forget is that the complexities of international affairs make simple solutions and trustworthy prophesies impossible. Here the scholar and the charlatan part company. Knowledge of the forces that determine politics among nations, and of the ways by which their political relations unfold, reveals the ambiguity of the facts of international politics."[3]

Imagining that the world is neatly predictable is precisely the sort of claim that the classical realists cautioned against – we want the world to be predictable, because a predictable world is more comfortable

---

[1] General critiques of the "scientific" or positivist turn in realist theory can be found in Ashley 1984; Walker 1987 and 1993; and Williams 2005.
[2] Morgenthau 1967, p. 4.   [3] Morgenthau 1967, p. 19.

to be in, and therefore we will go out and look for evidence that the world is so. A neatly predictable world is one in which we can construct policy edifices that manage our foreign relations successfully without our having to think about it much. A realist world is one in which we must carefully marshal our power, lest we abuse it without thinking, or lose it while not paying attention. To be clear, I am not making the argument in this chapter that realist theory is incompatible with drawing inferences from historical observation or data, or with using those inferences to make contingent predictions about what the results of given policy choices may be. Rather, I am making the argument that realist theory is incompatible with the epistemological assumption that international relations are fundamentally predictable, or that we should view them as if they are.

There are three ramifications of this observation, and of the logic of the social more broadly, for a realism that is not internally contradictory. The first is that in order to recover its roots as prescriptive theory, it must be wary of making claims of scientific prediction. The second is that if realism is to be prescriptive, it must be so as a theory of foreign policy, not a theory of systems structure. And the third is that power politics must have a normative context, for to have a theory of foreign policy (or of policy of any kind, for that matter) without a normative context is pointless. As a setting for discussion of these ramifications, though, I begin with the question of how realism changed from the contextualism of the classical realists to the scientific prediction of many (but certainly not all) realists today. This question can be addressed by looking at two debates that marked the development of the discipline of international relations in its first half-century or so, the first between realism and idealism, and the second between traditionalism and science.

Realism and the great debates

The history of the discipline of international relations is often told as a sequence of "great debates."[4] The first of these debates, occurring between the world wars and immediately after the Second World War, was between realism and idealism. In the conventional telling of the history, it was won by the realists. The second of these

[4] See, for example, Lapid 1989.

debates, dating primarily from the 1960s, was between traditional or historical approaches and science, and is often thought of as being won by the scientists, at least insofar as international relations as a discipline is practiced in the United States.[5] But one can also argue that this second debate in fact represented a loss for classical realism, and that the insight into international politics that underlay the seminal realist works in the 1930s and 1940s was lost in the field's attempt to become more scientific.

What we have come to think of as the first debate was, to a large extent, an exercise in caricature of Wilsonian liberal idealism by mid-twentieth-century realists, most clearly E. H. Carr, who characterized liberal idealism as utopianism.[6] However accurate the portrayal of Wilsonians and other idealist thinkers by the early realists, and however accurate the portrayal of the interwar discipline of international relations as a debate between these two groups, the exercise in caricature was effective.[7] From the realist perspective it was perhaps too effective, as will be discussed later in this chapter. The basic realist point in setting up Wilsonian liberal idealism as naïve utopianism was that we must understand the world the way that it is, rather than the way we would like it to be. And the way that it is, according to those seminal realists, is messy, historically contingent, and political. The caricature of Wilsonian idealism was that if we set up the right international institutions, if we get the formal structure of international politics right, then international relations becomes functional rather than political.[8] It becomes, in other words, predictable. The classical realists ridiculed liberal idealism as utopian precisely because of this conceit that politics could be made predictable.

The extent to which realism won the first debate is easy to overstate. Claims of realist victory ignore the prominent roles of functionalism, integration theory, and other approaches to the study of international relations that draw more heavily on the idealist rather than on the realist end of interwar thinking in the discipline. It also ignores the efforts put into the creation of international institutions in the postwar period. But the claim that realism won the first debate can also be misleading, because it implies that the core intuition of the realists of the time triumphed. While the language of realism has remained

[5] Lapid 1989.   [6] Carr 1964; Schmidt 1998.
[7] For example Barkin 2003a, p. 332.   [8] For example Morgenthau 1967, p. 3.

a central feature of the contemporary discipline of international relations, however, this core intuition has not.

It is easy to think of the second debate, between historical and scientific approaches to the study of international relations, as orthogonal to the first. One might even think that realism belonged on the side of science, given Hans Morgenthau's invocation of laws of nature in support of realism.[9] But to focus on this phrase is to miss the core point of Morgenthau's critique of liberal idealism, a point suggested by the title of his 1946 book, *Scientific Man Versus Power Politics*.[10] In referring to "scientific man," Morgenthau is speaking of the sort of liberal idealism and scientific humanism often associated with political scientists in the tradition of Woodrow Wilson.[11] The essence of this school of thought is that people have consistent and reasonable (or at least predictable) preferences, which they pursue rationally.[12] As a result, well-designed political institutions within which people can rationally pursue their preferences in a way that interferes as little as possible with the abilities of others to do so will appeal sufficiently to people's reasonableness as to obviate any necessity for power politics. The universalization of these institutions, for the liberal idealist, can insure perpetual peace by eliminating the causes of war.[13]

The classical realist response is that no ultimate solutions are available. "Peace is subject to the conditions of time and space and must be established and maintained by different methods and under different conditions of urgency in the every-day relations of concrete nations. The problem of international peace as such exists only for the philosopher."[14] That is, the right institutions can deal successfully with particular political problems at a particular time and place, but this nexus of problem, time, and place is historically unique; there will inevitably be other problems in other times and places. To the extent that many, if not most, international political problems have

---

[9] Morgenthau 1967, p. 4.

[10] Morgenthau 1946.

[11] See, for example, Kegley 1993 and Schmidt 1998.

[12] A key difference between this school of thought and contemporary rationalist approaches in the study of IR is that in the latter the assumption of reasonableness falls out. People are assumed to be instrumentally rational, but are not necessarily assumed to respect the rights and well-being of others when to do so would not be demonstrably instrumentally rational.

[13] The phrase "perpetual peace" is from Kant 1957.

[14] Morgenthau 1946, p. 217.

at least some distributional ramifications, the relative gains or prefer-
ential distributions in the solutions to new problems, or problems in
different times and places, will likely reflect the interests of the actors
best able to stake their claim to those gains, that is, the actors with
the greater power. As such, no matter how well designed the structure
of political institutions, political power will always be the ultimate
arbiter of outcomes in international politics.

The second debate was, in effect, about the same division that
Morgenthau was speaking of. The debate pitted those who thought of
international relations as a science against those who thought of it as
an art. The former group argued that good research into international
relations should be systematic, and that the results should be falsifia-
ble. That, in other words, we should be looking at patterned regulari-
ties in international politics, rather than erudite musings on specific
events. The international-relations-as-history side responded that such
patterns are ephemeral at best, misleading at worst.[15] The "science"
side of the debate, in other words, fit neatly into Morgenthau's category of scientific man. When Morgenthau spoke of power politics,
on the other hand, he was speaking as well of historical contingency.

As such, Morgenthau was clearly on the side of the traditionalists
in this debate, as were other seminal realists.[16] But realism as a whole,
understood as a self-identifying group of scholars, bifurcated, and
over time the majority of the realist disciplinary community in the
United States came to lean toward the science end of the debate (the
opposite was true in the United Kingdom, with the development of
the English school of international relations theory[17]). The process by
which traditional realist concepts were translated into the language
of science is traced by Stephano Guzzini in *Realism in International
Relations and International Political Economy: The Continuing
Story of a Death Foretold*.[18] In this disciplinary community sense the
second debate was indeed orthogonal to the place of realism in the

---

[15] See, for example, Knorr and Rosenau 1969 for arguments from both sides
of this debate.
[16] For a more detailed examination of this claim, see Guzzini 1998.
[17] Hedley Bull, for example, was both a key player on the traditionalist
side of the second debate, and a seminal author of the English school of
international relations theory. See, for example, Knorr and Rosenau 1969;
and Bull 1977.
[18] Guzzini 1998, Chapter 3.

field of international relations – it did not directly affect the strength of the community of realist scholars within the discipline. But in another sense, the translation of mainstream realism in the United States into the language of "science," with its emphasis on the assumption of patterned behavior, undermined the core insight of the classical realists.

This is the case because the translation into the language of science implicates realist logic with precisely the same liberal idealist assumptions that the classical realists focused on opposing. The methods discussed as scientific in the science/traditionalism debate ranged from the statistical to the formal, from the inductive to the deductive, but they all have in common that they assume patterned human behavior. They assume people will react to given structural conditions either as they have in the past (in the case of statistical/inductive approaches) or in a manner consistent with a specific set of deductive assumptions about human behavior (as is the case with rational choice theory or systems theory). To the extent that human behavior is patterned, institutions can be designed around the pattern to yield desired political results. To the extent that the pattern holds, the institutions should continue to work. This logic is precisely that which Morgenthau defined as the "scientific man" approach to the study of politics (or, perhaps more accurately, of policy).[19] This is true whether the assumptions reflect the belief the people actually behave in the manner assumed, or is an "as if" assumption. In the latter case, the analogy with "scientific man" is even clearer, inasmuch as the assumption is about how we would like people to behave (in this case, for reasons of analytical rather than political tractability) rather than about how we think people do behave.

Many contemporary realists will no doubt look at the preceding paragraph and completely fail to recognize it as a description of what they do. They are more likely to see it as a description of neoliberal institutionalism (an approach which was originally proposed, we might recall, as a variant of neorealism, not as an exercise in liberal theory).[20] It applies, however, to much contemporary realist theorizing as well. Certainly not all – much of the recent work by neoclassical realists, while deploying the language of science, allows substantially more scope for agency than neorealist approaches.[21] But it does apply,

---

[19] Morgenthau 1946.   [20] Keohane 1984 and 1989.
[21] See, *inter alia*, Sterling-Folker 2009; and Lobell, Ripsman, and Taliaferro 2009.

for example, to game-theoretical approaches to realism, be those games expressed discursively, as with much work on the prisoners' dilemma,[22] or formally. To the extent that a game has a solution,[23] it obviates the practice of politics. It applies even more so to attempts to create systemic theories of realism, and in particular neorealism, as is discussed in the next section.

Classical realist logic, then, to the extent that it explicitly won the first great debate, implicitly lost the second. One could argue that it lost this debate because disciplinary international relations in the United States was generally located in political science departments that were participants in the behavioral revolution, because of physics (or economics) envy, or because social science in the United States has a fundamentally liberal view of the individual that gradually overcame the European perspectives of many of the seminal realists.[24] Whatever the explanation (and all of those noted here may well be contributing factors), the process of scientization of the discipline of international relations, particularly in the United States, marked a turning point for realism. It marked a point at which mainstream realism adopted a key ontological assumption that it had previously defined itself in contrast with. This in turn means that the systemic and rationalist realism that dominate the field now are, in important ways, founded on an internal contradiction.[25]

Prediction and description

At the core of this internal contradiction is the tension between prescriptive and predictive theory. Of course, there is no clear line between theories that can be used predictively and those that can be used prescriptively. In fact, in some senses the one presumes the other – prediction in social theory has little point if it cannot be used for some sort of policy prescription, and conversely policy prescription is less than credible if completely dissociated from predictions of

---

[22] E.g. Jervis 1978.
[23] "Solution" understood in this context as a stable (Nash) equilibrium.
[24] On this last possibility, see Sterling-Folker 2006a. See also Gunnell 1993; Walker 1993.
[25] Ashley 1984 argues that classical realism can do everything that neorealism can do, and more. I argue that classical realism cannot in fact do what neorealism claims to do, because the claim is itself internally contradictory.

outcome. But there is a difference in basic intent between two kinds of theory in international relations that I label here predictive and prescriptive.

What I am calling predictive theory is an approach to the study of international relations that begins with the premise that these politics are essentially patterned, and that social science should focus on establishing what the patterns are. Predictive theory can be used as a basis for policy prescription, but such prescription is in turn based on the assumption of continuity, of predictability, the assumption that the pattern will hold in current conditions to the same extent that it did in the past or in the model, unless there are clear indications that conditions in the current case differ from those in the past. It is an approach that is, in a fundamental way, non-recursive – it does not allow for the possibility that political actors will figure out the patterns and change their thinking accordingly. This is true even for rational choice approaches, despite their allowance for strategic interaction. Strategy in this sense allows actors to change their behavior in response to expectations of the behavior of the adversary, but does not allow for changes in identities and interests, let alone discursive structures, in response to given strategies.

Prescriptive theory is an approach that is grounded in a current policy issue or problem rather than in general patterns of behavior or outcome. It is, in this sense, problem-focused rather than pattern-focused. It is not based on the premise that political outcomes are predictable. Rather, it is based on the premise that context is sufficiently important that each policy setting is unique, and that the possibility of agency renders past patterns less than reliable guides to future expectations. Of course, prescriptive theory does not eschew inference from existing and past patterns in human affairs – to do so would be to leave no starting place for the analysis of specific policies, specific contexts. But prescriptive theory's emphasis on the uniqueness of any given context nonetheless remains in contrast with predictive theory's emphasis on the patterned.

Classical realism was prescriptive. The seminal realists of the mid-twentieth century argued that we cannot predict human behavior, both because of the inability to theorize agency and because of the need for reflexivity. Classical realists (Morgenthau more so than Carr) did argue that individuals seek power, and that from this observation some general patterns in international politics could be intuited. And they certainly argued (again, Morgenthau more than Carr) that we should, to the best of our ability, understand cause and effect relationships that make some outcomes more likely than others in specific political situations. But they did not argue that this general propensity for power-seeking could yield strong predictions about the actions of specific agents. The human disposition may be power-seeking, but in the absence of a thorough understanding of the political goals of other agents this disposition does not provide the basis for predicting behavior.

The inability to theorize agency suggests that it is precisely those actors who are most likely to act entrepreneurially, whose actions we are therefore least able to predict, that we should be most concerned about. Policy, in other words, should be cognizant of the unpredictable as well as the predictable. And reflexivity suggests that we cannot fully understand other actors. It suggests that we are likely to be projecting ourselves onto our study of others, and therefore that we should be modest in the extent to which we are willing to take such study as authoritative. As a result, classical realism prescribed prudence, prescribed a foreign policy in which we do not become over-confident about our knowledge of the world, of how other actors will respond to our foreign policy, and of what we can successfully accomplish in the world. "Realism, then, considers prudence – the weighing of the consequences of alternative political actions – to be the supreme virtue in international politics."[26] The prescription to be concerned with relative power in this context is a prescription to keep insurance against the unpredictability of our own power and of the behavior of others.

If the behavior of others can be reliably predicted, then institutional structures can be created to contain and constrain this behavior. This logic is how neoliberal institutionalism went from the same basic set of assumptions as Waltz's neorealism to a theory of effective international regimes.[27] It is also, to an extent, inherent in Waltz's neorealism as well. If bipolarity is stable because the logic of internal balancing dominates the logic of external balancing, then as long as we as a polar power internally balance the system will remain stable.[28] The institution of bipolarity thereby recreates itself without any need for thinking about foreign policy on an issue-by-issue basis. Foreign

---

[26] Morgenthau 1967, p. 10.   [27] Keohane 1984.
[28] Waltz 1979.

policy for a polar power in a bipolar system in this sense becomes irrelevant, as long as our military spending is calibrated in a way that maximizes power (whatever power means for Waltz[29]) over both the short and long terms. In fact, by this logic, any attempt at engaging in any foreign policy as a polar power is misguided, in that it distracts from internal balancing.

In their efforts to be scientific, some contemporary realists confuse prediction and prescription, and as a result fail on both counts. If we have a predictive theory that tells us that people will of their own accord act as power maximizers, then we do not need a prescriptive theory to tell our foreign policy decision-makers to act as power balancers or maximizers. By way of comparison, rational choice theorists do not feel the need to tell people to act rationally. They assume that people do act rationally (or that their behavior can be understood as if they were behaving rationally), and then tell decision-makers how to design institutions to allow for this assumed individually rational behavior in a way that will maximize aggregate utility. But many contemporary realists argue that decision-makers will, as a matter of course, act rationally to maximize power, and feel the need at the same time to exhort decision-makers to act rationally to maximize power, implying that otherwise these decision-makers might act differently.[30] Herein lies the internal contradiction.

Contemporary approaches to the study of international relations that draw both from the realist side of the realism/idealism debate and the science side of the science/history debate, then, risk failure both as predictive and as prescriptive theory. To the extent that they accept the core insight of classical realism, they fail as predictive theory in their own terms, and for the same reasons that classical realism did not attempt to predict – the constraints of the logic of the social and of agency, and the need for reflexivity. In other words, Morgenthau's critique of "scientific man" in the study of politics applies to "scientific" approaches to realism as much as it does to the liberal idealism to which Morgenthau applied it.

---

[29] Waltz identifies power with the distribution of capabilities (as opposed to Dahl's idea of power as control), but never clearly defines capabilities. Waltz 1979, pp. 191–192. See also Dahl 1961.

[30] See, for example, the advertisement in the *New York Times* against invading Iraq, signed by a veritable who's-who of leading international relations scholars. New York Times 2002.

And these approaches fail as prescriptive theory because once one has claimed an ability to accurately predict the behaviors and responses of others, the logic for power maximization as policy prescription has failed. Take as an example the work of John Mearsheimer, a leading proponent of offensive realism, a contemporary attempt at realist theorizing that combines Waltz's structuralism with Morgenthau's view of human nature.[31] Offensive realism predicts that great powers will always strive to achieve hegemony. At the same time, Mearsheimer is also active in the area of policy prescription, for example publicly arguing against the US invasion of Iraq in 2003.[32] But if great powers are always going to act in a certain way, what is the point of policy prescription?

Ido Oren develops this argument in detail, and effectively rebuts Mearsheimer's arguments that his predictions and prescriptions are epistemologically compatible.[33] Mearshiemer's way out of his dilemma is to claim that prediction does not always work, so that realists need occasionally to remind policy-makers of what they need to do. But, as Oren points out, this argument fails on two counts. First, a theory of war that does not predict reliably, and that does not tell us when it is unlikely to be reliable, is in fact not of much use in a science of international relations. And second, realists have been disagreeing with US foreign policy consistently for over half a century. This is not an occasional failure of realist prediction, it is a systematic failure.

The logic of offensive realism raises a further question with respect to the distinction between prediction and prescription. Mearsheimer argues that great powers will attempt to become hegemons, but he also argues that they will almost always fail.[34] As a matter of prescription, he argues that great powers should maximize power, to balance the power maximization of the other great powers that will necessarily behave that way.[35] But they will fail – Mearsheimer tells us that they usually do. So why do we need to try, if only to balance others who will fail anyway? The conflation of prediction (we will strive for hegemony) and goal (we should strive for hegemony) is a theoretical sleight-of-hand that puts us precisely in the sort of

[31] Mearsheimer 2001.
[32] A list of his public affairs commentary can be found at http://mearsheimer. uchicago.edu/pub-affairs.html (accessed March 15, 2009).
[33] Oren 2009.
[34] Mearsheimer 2001, for example p. 35.   [35] Mearsheimer 2001.

recursive situation that E. H. Carr warned about in *The Twenty Years' Crisis*, in which our fears create their own reality.[36] If we will strive for hegemony because great powers always do so, then offensive realist policy prescription should be unnecessary. If we must strive for hegemony because otherwise other great powers might achieve it, then the theory's prediction has failed. If we strive for hegemony because we confuse power with political goals, then we will probably create the security threat that we were trying to protect ourselves against in the first place.

Realism and foreign policy

One of the key ramifications of realism's relationship with predictive theory is that the translation to systems theory necessarily loses the core insights of the classical realists. Their injunction to see the world as it is calls for a realism that is, at heart, a theory of foreign policy, not a theory of systemic constraints. Realism understood as such fails as systems theory because systems theories, or at least those constructed by self-described political realists, are about constraints, patterns, and self-replication. They are about constraints in the same way that any structural theory is about constraints on agency – they posit that the system limits what agents can do successfully, that it constrains the range of options open to actors. These constraints create patterns in international politics, and these patterns can be counted upon. The patterns, and the systems that create them, are also self-replicating, in the sense that they recreate the same set of constraints on political actors no matter what those actors do. There is no room for agency in such a system.

This is not to say that there is necessarily anything wrong with this kind of systems theory. Rather, it is to say that it is incompatible with the argument of classical realists that international politics are contingent, and that agency matters. Attempts to combine realist logic and systems theory in the end come to resemble the sort of theory that Morgenthau critiqued as liberal idealism in *Scientific Man*,[37] because these attempts end up relying on liberal mechanisms to explain why and how the system self-replicates. These mechanisms are liberal in the sense that they are institutions that, given certain conditions of

---

[36] Carr 1964, p. 89.   [37] Morgenthau 1946.

possibility, operate as self-equilibrating social institutions, in which individuals acting in their own interests end up maintaining a social system as an incidental effect. In other words, liberal in the sense that they serve to obviate politics.

As an example, Deborah Boucoyannis argues that Waltz's neorealism is in fact a liberal theory inasmuch as it relies on the logic of that ultimate liberal institution, the market. In Waltz's systems theory, individual states act to secure their own interests by maximizing their own power, but the nature of the system transforms these individually maximizing behaviors into a stable balance of power. Those states that do not compete effectively go out of business. The balance of power in this theory works in the same way as the market works in economic theory, as an invisible hand that transforms individual maximizing behavior into a stable and efficient social system.[38]

One might respond that the balance of power is a core concept of realist theory.[39] But it would be more accurate to say that there is a concept of balance of power that is a core concept of realist theory. It has long since been noted that there are a variety of uses of the phrase "balance of power."[40] In fact, Morgenthau in the course of one book, *Politics Among Nations*, uses it in no fewer than four quite different ways.[41] One of the common ways in which the term is used is in reference to a specific historical system, in nineteenth-century Europe. The term can also be used to indicate that at any point in time there is a distribution of power across states, without implying that it was necessarily in a particular balance (e.g. the balance of power after the fall of the Iron Curtain strongly favored the United States).

Waltz uses the term in a third way, not as a generic reference to the distribution of power across states, but to refer to a specific sort of distribution, one in which no great power is able to concentrate sufficient power to change the structure of the system.[42] This usage is very different from the previous one – the generic usage does not imply a self-replicating system, an invisible hand of some kind, whereas the latter does. Nor does it imply any necessary activity on the part of individual states to maintain the balance. In fact, Waltz specifically

---

[38] Boucoyannis 2007.
[39] For a review of the status of the concept in contemporary realism see Nexon 2009.
[40] Claude 1962.   [41] Morgenthau 1967, pp. 161.
[42] Waltz 1979, pp. 117–123.

claims that his is not a theory of foreign policy.[43] But the fourth common usage of the phrase "balance of power" is specifically in reference to foreign policy. It is, in fact, a foreign policy, one in which a state works self-consciously to balance the power of other states (or other social institutions) that it finds threatening. And it is in this use that the phrase becomes a core concept of classical realism.[44]

The key differences between balance-of-power as a self-regulating system and balance-of-power as a foreign policy are prescription and agency – the difference between something a decision-maker can choose to do or not do, and something that happens by itself (the other two uses of the phrase noted above both fall into the category of description, and are therefore orthogonal to the distinction that I am making here). Classical realist arguments were about what foreign-policy decision-makers needed to do to achieve their goals in international politics. Balancing power is, in this context, a strategy that creates latitude for achieving goals by improving a state's relative political position. As a prescription, the concept of balance of power used in this meaning is a good example of the way in which classical realist logic respects agency in ways that attempts at a more scientific approach to realism do not. It respects the agency of the decision-maker being exhorted to balance power, for a decision-maker without agency need not be exhorted. And it also respects the agency of decision-makers in other states, by assuming that we must balance against the unexpected, not against a particular predicted foreign policy by others.

The classical realist conclusion of balance-of-power as policy prescription marks a point of disjuncture with most of the emerging body of literature that describes itself as neoclassical realist. Although this latter literature explicitly focuses on the study of foreign policy, it does so for the most part in a descriptive rather than prescriptive way. Neoclassical realists take the assumption of structural realism, that there is an objective optimal foreign policy dictated by the international balance of power (understood in systemic terms), and look to domestic factors to explain deviations from this ideal.[45] This intervention of domestic politics in the foreign policy-making process

---

[43] Waltz 1979, p. 121.
[44] Guzzini 1998, p. 46. See also Claude 1962.
[45] For example Rose 1998; Schweller 2003; and Lobell, Ripsman, and Taliaferro 2009.

allows little scope for prescription – it assumes that policy-makers know of the ideal, and cannot achieve it. In any case, the neoclassical approach, in building from a neorealist rather than classical realist worldview, loses both the reflexivity and the respect for agency that is to be found in classical realist thinking.

That realist logic is basically that of a prescriptive theory of foreign policy has implications for the relationship between realism and constructivism, two of which are the comparative understandings of power between the two approaches, and the relative place of normative theory in the two approaches. The implication with respect to power is that realism's understanding of the concept is necessarily narrower than constructivism's, to the extent that realism is a theory of foreign policy.

The discussion of realism and power politics in Chapter 2 noted that realism's use of the term is relative, relational, and social. But it is also interactional. Michael Barnett and Raymond Duvall distinguish between interactional power and constitutional power. The former "treats social relations as comprised of the actions of preconstituted social actors toward one another,"[46] while in the latter case "power works through social relations that analytically precede the social or subject positions of actors."[47] As they note, realism has traditionally biased the use of the term in the discipline of international relations toward interaction, and away from constitutional power. This bias is inevitable in a theory of foreign policy – to the extent that realism is prescriptive, it focuses on what specific actors should do. As such, its prescriptive concept of power is inherently about interactions, about what individual policy-makers and agentive social institutions can do to maximize their own power. The focus on interactional power, however, is also a source of weakness for realist thinking, if it prevents realists from recognizing constitutional power, and the limits that constitutional power can place on agency. A reflexive realism, therefore, should recognize constitutional power even as it focuses on interactional power. It is to avoid the bias that Barnett and Duvall point to, and to leave space for the reflexive recognition of constitutional power, that I use the phrase "power politics," rather than simply "power," in association with realism.

---

[46] Barnett and Duvall 2005, p. 45.   [47] Barnett and Duvall 2005, p. 46.

The second implication of the foreign-policy orientation inherent in realist logic for the relationship between it and constructivist logic is that the orientation implies different relationships between each approach on the one hand and normative international relations theory on the other. The demands of reflexivity are similar for both approaches – in either case scholars need to be cognizant of the normative biases, presuppositions, and assumptions that they bring to their studies. But beyond reflexivity, realism has a much more direct, necessary, and dialectical relationship with normative theory than does constructivism.

Realism and normative theory

This claim, that realist logic has a much closer relationship with normative theory than does constructivist, may at first glance seem odd, given realism's focus on power politics and its traditional self-description as being an alternative to (and analytically superior to) idealism. It may also seem odd given constructivism's focus on norms and ideas, terms that are strikingly similar to normative theory and idealism. But this terminological similarity in the latter instance should not be taken to indicate a necessary relationship, and what seems a categorical opposition in the first instance is in fact a much more nuanced relationship than at first appears to be the case.

A good place to start in the terminological distinction is with Alex Wendt. He notes that "[e]ver since Carr's devastating critique, 'idealist' has functioned in IR primarily as an epithet for naivete."[48] He makes this point before distinguishing between idealism as a theory of social politics and Idealism (which he capitalizes) as a theory of IR. The first idealism refers to social theory that looks at the importance of ideas, whereas the second refers to a theory of IR based on ideals rather than on realism. Wendt makes the claim that he is involved in doing the former, looking at ideas, not the latter. Whether or not this claim is accurate is debatable, but the claim itself points to a distinction between an approach to the study of international relations that looks at the role of ideas about what international politics should look like, and an approach that begins with an assumed idea of what international politics should look like. The same observation could

[48] Wendt 1999, p. 33.

be made about the difference between the study of norms (in which norms are the object of study) and normative studies (in which a particular normative position is applied to a political question).

In noting this distinction, Wendt is trying to rehabilitate the term "idealism" from the conception that it represents a normative approach to social science, that it is focused on ideology rather than empirics. He is in effect trying to liberate the label of idealism from normative associations in an attempt to create "scientific" and, presumably therefore, value-free, social science.[49] Interestingly, in *The Twenty Years' Crisis*, Carr does not use the term "idealism" at all; instead, he speaks of utopianism, while Morgenthau speaks of liberalism and of scientific man. But although the terms that Carr and Morgenthau employed seem quite different, both were, in fact, referring to normative approaches to the study of international relations. This would seem to put classical realist and constructivist logic on the same page with respect to normative approaches, rejecting them in favor of the study of the world as it is. And the core classical realist claim is that in the world as it is what matters is power politics.

But as we have already seen, the classical realists recognized that political power and political morality exist in a necessary and dialectical relationship with each other. In fact, Chapter 6 of *The Twenty Years' Crisis* bears a title almost identical to that of this chapter, and is entirely devoted to making the argument that a foreign policy not guided by a moral sense is pointless.[50] Michael Williams argues that an ethic of responsibility lies at the core of the classical realist tradition.[51] In short, classical realists viewed their efforts as a necessary corrective to idealism, but not as a replacement. Idealism, for the classical realist, is necessary to inform our actions and underlie our interests in the pursuit of international politics, but realism will always remain a necessary part of relations among states. Herein lies the difference between realists on the one hand and "utopians" or "scientific men" on the other. Whereas the latter believe that we can ultimately build a world politics not based on power, the realist believes that we cannot. For those classical realists, however well designed our international institutions, however well aligned our national interests, and however well intentioned our ideas, power politics will remain the

[49] Wendt 1999, p. 39.   [50] Carr 1964, pp. 89–94.
[51] Williams 2005.

ultimate arbiter (note, not the ultimate source) of outcomes. Because neither human nature nor human institutions are ultimately perfectible, we will always have to remain both diligent in identifying those who would subvert the system to their own ends and in remaining capable of dealing with them effectively for our ends.

A corollary of this argument is the observation that without addressing "the compromise between power and morality" we cannot successfully address the phenomenon of political change.[52] This inability to account for change is one of the standard charges leveled against neorealism, particularly Waltz's variety.[53] In this sense, Waltz has come full circle to meet the Wilsonian idealists who provided the foil for both Carr and Morgenthau. Waltz's theory of the structure of power, without scope for morality, becomes static in the same way that theories of the structure of morality without power do. Neither pure realism nor pure idealism can account for political change, only the interplay of the two, subject to the assumption that morality is contextual rather than universal. And because morality is neither absolute nor perfectible, the moral choices of agents cannot be entirely predictable. Therefore in realist logic a key space for agency, and hence a key source of change, in international politics is to be found in the dialectical relationship between power and morality.

Because morality in realist logic is contextual, not all uses of power, even when in the interest of a moral ideal, will be compatible, because not all moral ideals are compatible. Even if all actors in the international system at a given point in time accept the same basic set of normative structures, they will differ in their interpretations of those structures, whether for rationally self-interested reasons or for psychological reasons,[54] or because of the complexity and room for interpretation within any moral system. When interpretations differ, the power of the interpreter continues to matter. The realist dialectic of power and morality accepts that morality should underlie foreign policy, but it is nonetheless skeptical of any claims to moral universality.

In this moral skepticism lies a key difference between idealist and realist arguments. Idealists recognize a single ideal, a universal

---

[52] Carr 1964, p. 210.
[53] Two examples of such a charge can be found in Ruggie 1983 and Walker 1987.
[54] See, for example, Jervis 1976; Rosati 2000; and Shannon 2000.

political morality toward which we should strive. Classical realists argued that no universal political morality exists and, therefore, if we want ours to triumph, we must arrange to have it do so through the application of power. But the classical realists, particularly Carr, warn us that the relationship can be used both ways: morality can also be used as a tool of power. So that when we apply power to promote our preferred political morality, others might see it as a use of power simply to promote our interests. Political psychology suggests, furthermore, that when we justify a use of power to ourselves as being for moral purposes, we may simply be fooling ourselves and rationalizing an action as moral that we want to take for other reasons.[55] As such, even though power politics is hollow without political morality, the classical realist argument is that we must, nonetheless, apply to moral claims, ours reflexively as well as those of others, a certain skepticism when morality is used to justify power politics.

Stated as such, classical realist logic begins to sound much like certain kinds of critical theory as applied in IR.[56] Parts of Carr's *The Twenty Years' Crisis*, in fact, sound like a Foucauldian critique of Wilsonian idealism.[57] These sections include the argument that political actions in the international domain, even when motivated by the best of intentions, have ramifications on the distribution of power that can affect both the ultimate effectiveness of the actions and the way those actions are viewed by others. Thus for Carr the League of Nations, even if it was created by the status quo powers to promote international peace, was viewed by others as an exercise in supporting the relative power of the states that created it. And the same can happen as well to any international institution, even if created with the best of intentions.

Conclusion

Realist logic, in other words, to the extent that it is derived from a core concept of power politics, works best as a theory of foreign policy, and makes no sense if divorced from all political morality. Marrying realist logic and the demands of an epistemology of social science that sees the world as predictable creates internal contradictions that

[55] See, for example, Jervis 1976.   [56] See, for example, Ashley 1984.
[57] On which, see Ashley and Walker 1990; Der Derian 1990; and Walker 1993.

the proponents of such a move seem unable to work out or to finesse. Classical realism argued that in order to most effectively promote our political morality through our foreign policy, we need to be cognizant of the constraints of power politics in an anarchical world. And we need to be cognizant of the fact that political morality is not universal. In other words, we need to be reflexive in our study of international politics. Finally, we need to allow for agency in our interactions with other countries – we must not assume that we can predict accurately how others will respond to our foreign policy.

Constructivist logic would seem a useful corrective to the predictive turn that much of realism has been taking since the 1960s, since the time of the second great debate. It gives us a framework within which to study the relationship of agent to international political structure, as well as a set of methods with which to do so. Those methods are useful for exploring the relationship between norms and power politics in international relations, and the relationship between norms and normative theory. And it shares a similar reflexivity to that demanded by classical realism. But, like realism, constructivism has its own limits, and these are the subject of the next chapter.

9 | *The limits of constructivism*

Constructivism, like realism, loses its point if stretched too far. For realism, this stretching has historically been in the direction of "science," in an attempt to make a prescriptive theory of foreign policy into both predictive and systems theory. There are two key areas in which constructivism threatens to be stretched too far. One is in the direction of normative theory. And the other is that the term, and the concept, simply risks being spread too thin. One can think of this as a sort of diluting of the constructivist brand – if everything is constructivism, then being constructivist does not get you far.

Being stretched too thin draws on a number of points made in earlier chapters, particularly Chapters 2, 3, and 4, discussing definitions, materialism, and the logic of the social, respectively. At its most simple, the risk is that if everything that is not strictly both materialist and rationalist is defined as constructivist, then the term comes to cover almost all work in the discipline of international relations. This may be a useful political move for constructivists attempting to establish a stronger position within the discipline, but it can be a counterproductive move communicatively, because the term "constructivism," if it applies to everyone, loses any real meaning.

Before the discussion of stretching constructivism too thin, this chapter will begin by revisiting the relationship between constructivism and normative theory. The last chapter ended with a claim that constructivist logic should be able to help realist research with the relationship between approaches to the study of international relations that look at norms on the one hand, and normative approaches on the other. But there have been a number of suggestions so far in this book that the relationship between constructivism and normative approaches to the study of international relations is somewhat fraught. In particular, constructivism's relationship with liberalism, one of the predominant normative approaches in international relations theory in the United States, is problematic. How can these various observations be reconciled?

Constructivism and normative theory

Whereas realist approaches can run into difficulty if they eschew a commitment to political morality entirely, constructivist approaches risk running into an internal contradiction if they commit to a particular political morality non-problematically. In practice, this is an issue particularly with respect to the relationship between constructivism and normative liberalism, primarily but not exclusively in the United States. This is by no means an argument against constructivist research that focuses on liberal norms, or that is undertaken to the end of promoting liberal norms. It is not, in other words, against constructivist work that is informed by normatively liberal political commitments. Rather, it is an argument against work that purports to be constructivist, yet at the same time assumes liberal norms as objectively privileged in the construction of international politics. This objective privileging can be either in the form of an assumption that liberal norms will in the absence of coercive power win out over other social constructions of political morality because they are inherently preferable, or in the form of assumptions about the perfectibility of human nature. Note that this discussion of privileging applies to any particular normative structure. I have used liberalism rather than other normative approaches as an example both because liberalism as political ideology tends toward the hegemonic in American academia,[1] and because attempts to combine constructivism with it are more widespread in disciplinary international relations in the United States than attempts to combine constructivism with other normative assumptions.

Two specific tendencies toward liberal idealism in the work of self-described contemporary constructivists serve to illustrate the potentially problematic relationship between it and normative liberalism.[2] The first tendency involves choosing to study issue areas compatible

[1] See, for example, Sterling-Folker 2006a.
[2] The purpose of this discussion is not to imply that those included are more important or central to constructivist theory than those not included – the selection is, in this sense, not systematic.

with liberal idealism in relatively non-critical ways. The second is to use as philosophical touchstones theorists of a liberal-idealist bent.

We cannot, of course, reasonably ascribe a normative bias to a methodological approach based on the topical foci of some of its practitioners. However, we can note a tendency to approach certain types of issues in a non-self-critical fashion. The fact that many of the well-known mainstream constructivists focus on issues like human rights,[3] security communities,[4] or multilateralism[5] does not make them unreflective in their liberal idealism. Rather, it is the way in which they focus on such issues that makes them so. Illustrating with the first of these issues, constructivists who write about human rights generally look at the role of international civil society, however understood,[6] as changing the behavior of states for the better. They are engaged in applied constructivism – intersubjective norms affect definitions of interest. But it is also liberal-idealist, in the sense that these norms are accepted largely uncritically as good ones, as are the elements of international civil society involved in spreading these norms.

Similarly, we cannot reasonably ascribe a normative bias to a methodological approach based on the theoretical antecedents upon which some of its practitioners draw. But to the extent that constructivists in the United States draw on the work of political theorists (as opposed to that of the social theorists upon whom they draw methodologically and epistemologically), these theorists often have liberal-idealist leanings. A good example is Wendt. He claims to accept the role of power in international relations and, thus, the basic realist premise as defined here. But he also argues, with reference to Kant, that the endogenous dynamic of international anarchy is progressive. In other words, absent exogenous shock, the culture of anarchy will tend to evolve from the Hobbesian world of enemies to the Lockean world of rivals and, ultimately, to the Kantian world of friends.[7] Once we have

---

[3] Sikkink 1993; Klotz 1995; Keck and Sikkink 1998; Risse, Ropp, and Sikkink 1999; and Burgerman 2001.

[4] Adler and Barnett 1998.   [5] Ruggie 1993.

[6] Sikkink 1993 speaks of principled issue-networks, Keck and Sikkink 1998 of advocacy networks, and Burgerman 2001 simply of activists. None would likely object to having what they are studying characterized as an element of global civil society. Burgerman speaks uncritically both of the activist community and of multilateralism.

[7] Wendt 1999, pp. 308–312.

arrived in the Kantian "role relationship" of friend,[8] international politics is unlikely to regress. Changing the social construction of anarchy can thereby obviate the worry that our neighbors will become enemies or rivals.

Another example, one less focused on American scholars than the others given here, involves constructivist research that draws on the work of Jürgen Habermas.[9] Using ideas such as communicative rationality, Habermas argues that communicative action and a well-structured public sphere can be an emancipatory force. He is generally identified as a critical theorist, but in certain respects he is a liberal idealist. Idealist in the sense that he has a clear notion of what constitutes political progress and the political good life, and liberal in the sense that this notion of the political good life is based on individual self-expression and a form of rationality (albeit not an instrumental rationality). Constructivist research that draws on Habermasian theory cannot easily separate the social theory (public spheres matter) from the normative theory (public spheres are good).

To be sure, neither of these tendencies – to choose particular issue areas or to rely on philosophical touchstones sympathetic to the liberal-idealist project – is universal. For example, Rodney Bruce Hall speaks explicitly of legitimacy as power; Martha Finnemore takes liberal theory to task for its ideological commitments.[10] Perhaps, more telling, most of the constructivists discussed above work or publish in the United States; it is probably both fairer and more accurate to ascribe the liberal-idealist tendency mostly to US constructivism, not constructivism more broadly[11] (for surveys of constructivist theory by scholars not working in the United States, see Ralph Pettman, and Karen Fierke and Knud Erik Jørgensen[12]). The relationship between US constructivism and liberal idealism itself is something that a realist constructivist approach might do well to examine.

[8] Wendt 1999, p. 309.
[9] For example, Linklater 1990 and 1998; Lynch 1999; Risse 2000.
[10] Finnemore 1996a; Hall 1997.
[11] Sterling-Folker 2006a provides a context for this claim by examining the liberal roots of American social science more broadly. Steele 2007 argues against the idea that this liberal strain is to be found in American constructivism.
[12] Pettman 2000; Fierke and Jørgensen 2001.

Research that assumes the normative primacy of liberal norms, as is often the case in these examples, is distinct from efforts to trace empirically the construction of liberal norms in international politics, and arguments about how to most effectively encourage the construction of these norms.[13] Such efforts are entirely compatible with constructivism to the extent that they recognize that social construction is intersubjective, that there is nothing objectively driving the adoption of liberal rather than other norms. They are similarly compatible to the extent that they recognize that liberal norms (as is the case with all norms) require continuous recreation through practice, and absent such recreation will likely evolve into other norms.[14]

There is, in other words, an incompatibility between constructivist logic and an empirically teleological understanding of any particular normative structure.[15] An understanding of a normative structure is empirically teleological when it assumes that the presence of this structure at a particular time and place will necessarily lead to a particular outcome. In the case of the examples noted above, this outcome is variously the adoption of liberal norms, or the conduct of politics through reasoned discourse. In either case, the creation of a normatively liberal set of political practices creates a virtuous circle that continues to reinforce those practices. But the core premise of constructivism is that normative structures are socially constructed, and can be socially re- or deconstructed. Structures are constraining on agency, but are not determinative. In other words, from a constructivist perspective there is no reason to assume the virtuous circle underlying the teleology.[16]

---

[13] For example Bernstein 2001.

[14] The discussion here emphasizes norms rather than rules or discourses. This follows the tendency for liberal constructivism, particularly in the United States, to be of the thin, or neoclassical, variants and to speak in terms of norms. The relationship holds true with liberal discourse as well.

[15] There is an even greater incompatibility between constructivism and teleological arguments based on claims of objective material conditions, for fairly straightforward reasons. For an example of such an argument, see Deudney 2006.

[16] For an argument in favor of teleological argument in international relations theory, see Wendt 2003. It is interesting to note that he predicts a world state in both Wendt 1994 and Wendt 2003. In the former, he self-identifies as a constructivist, and makes clear that he is not making teleological claims. By 2003, he is explicitly making teleological claims, but is no longer identifying his argument as constructivist.

A constructivist logic informed by a normatively liberal teleology is problematic, then, in a way that a constructivist logic informed by a normatively liberal political commitment is not. But by the same token, a realist logic informed by a normatively liberal political commitment is also perfectly reasonable. The realist argument is against those who would believe that liberal norms can replace politics, rather than those who believe in liberal political values. Like classical realism, constructivist research can be motivated by normative commitments, but must be informed by the realization that those commitments are not universal. Like realists, constructivists can believe absolutely in the value of the political norms to which they are committed, as long as they recognize that this absolute value is subjective, not intersubjective. This is the difference between a normative commitment and an empirical assumption. It would be naïve to expect that any research in international relations, whatever its claims to objectivity, is not colored by the former. But the empirical study of norms can be badly undermined by the latter.

Ultimately, the difference between a normative and a constructivist approach to the study of international politics is that the former is trying to promote the use of a particular normative structure, while the latter is trying to find out which normative and discursive structures predominate in a particular historical context. These are entirely compatible activities for a given scholar to undertake. Yet they are nonetheless distinct activities both epistemologically and methodologically, and as such the arguments of both are clearest, both conceptually and communicatively, when they are kept analytically distinct. Constructivism and normative analysis are in this sense in a dialectical relationship with each other. The relationship is not as specific as it is in the case of classical realist logic and normative theory, because the realist's policy orientation requires a clearer specification of normative position. But the general nature of the relationship as dialectic is similar.

Theory imperialism

These arguments suggest a clear disjuncture between normative and social constructivist approaches to the study of international relations, which in turn suggests a clear limit to constructivist logic. This limit is defined by the need to keep normative theorizing and constructivist empirical explanation both argumentatively and methodologically distinct from each other (although this by no means implies that both cannot be done by the same scholar, or within the same work). This need distinguishes constructivist approaches from those such as liberalism on the one hand and critical theory on the other.[17] But there are other limits to constructivism as well. One of these is suggested by the argument that the term does better service to the study of international relations as a distinct approach, rather than as a theory empire that attempts to bring as broad a range of approaches within its orbit as possible.

Chapter 2 discusses a number of ways to go about defining such approaches, including the expansive and the big-tent, as well as the weaknesses of these ways. It notes that big-tent definitions are more about disciplinary sociology than about the study of politics, and that expansive definitions tend both to dilute the usefulness of the term in conveying specific information about an approach, and to be exclusionary of those who do not fit within. Chapters 3 and 4 discuss the problems with the materialism/idealism and the consequences/appropriateness dichotomies as bases for defining constructivism. The result is a definition of constructivism based on intersubjectivity and the co-constitution of agents and structures. Such a definition would exclude an array of work, including, for example, work that looks at the role of ideas in international relations but not from a particularly intersubjectivist perspective, or work that begins with the premise that international politics are socially constructed, but that then looks only at the role of structure or agent in that construction, rather than the dialectical relationship of the two, even if such work self-identified as constructivist. Exclusion in this case would not imply that these works are any less valuable in the study of international relations, but rather that only labeling them constructivist is not particularly useful.

This narrower form of definition, conversely, does serve two useful functions, both of them already alluded to above. The first of these functions might be thought of as protecting the theory brand, and the second as avoiding theory imperialism. By protecting the brand, I mean insuring that the term "constructivism" actually conveys useful information about the methodology, epistemology, and ontology of an argument. The more expansive the definition, the less useful it is in this sense. One might respond that an expansive definition is useful

---

[17] See Hoffmann 2009.

as another kind of brand, a disciplinary or political one, in which the label of constructivism indicates affinity with a particular group of scholars in the profession, or with a political stance.[18] But in the first case, the label would not be necessarily related to any particular theoretical approach, so there is no reason to associate it with a term that has its origins in specifically such an approach. To do so is misleading. And in the second case, the political stance is probably better served by being described in its own terms, rather than camouflaged in epistemology.

The brand of constructivism, therefore, is best suited to a specific approach to the study of international relations grounded in a certain type of social theory, rather than to specific politics, be the politics disciplinary or international.[19] The arguments in Chapters 3 and 4 suggest that this theory is best stated in its own terms, in terms of intersubjectivity and co-creation, rather than as dichotomous oppositions that do justice neither to constructivism nor to those approaches with which it is being contrasted. To claim the label of constructivism for work that does not fit within the constraints of this theory betrays either intellectual laziness or a disciplinary political agenda.

The other danger is theory imperialism, by which I mean a process whereby an approach to the study of international relations begins to crowd out other approaches. To the extent, for example, that research labeled "constructivism" is easier to get into mainstream journals, particularly in the United States, than research labeled "critical theory," there is a professional incentive for scholars to label their research constructivist rather than critical.[20] Such relabeling may not have any effect on the actual content of any given piece of research, but at the margins it is likely to push the overall tenor of debate in the field toward the core premises of constructivism, and away from those of the competitor approaches that are being displaced. Theory imperialism in this sense does not necessarily refer to a conscious effort by

[18] See, for example, the use of constructivism as a disciplinary brand in Houghton 2007.

[19] See, for example, Onuf 1989, e.g. pp. 24–27, who sees constructivism as social codification rather than international theory.

[20] For example, in what is arguably the most prestigious academic general IR journal in the United States, *International Organization* (Giles and Garand 2007), in the five years prior to the writing of this footnote (volumes 56–60), "constructivism" appeared in titles or abstracts of articles 12 times (out of 136 articles). Critical theory did not appear even once.

practitioners of an approach at imperialism – the same effect, of one approach displacing others, can happen absent intentionality.

There are two problematic effects of theory imperialism, other than the issue of imprecision already alluded to. The first of these effects is a narrowing of possibilities. To the extent that a wide variety of specific approaches to the study of international relations is replaced by a much smaller set, and *in extremis* by the trichotomy of realism, liberalism, and constructivism, the range of possible approaches available to those who want to think about international relations is narrower. And to the extent that the approach taken delimits both the discourses available and the conclusions reached, this narrowing impoverishes our understanding of international relations. It limits the variety of ways available in which to think about specific issues, and limits the scope for cross-fertilization across different approaches. Whether or not methodological pluralism in the social sciences is a good thing is a subject of much contemporary debate, to which I will not contribute here.[21] But to the extent that one believes at minimum that some pluralism can be a good thing, a narrowing of possibilities is worrying.

The second of the problematic effects of theory imperialism is the marginalization of those aspects of other approaches that do not fit well into the imperial theory. Take as an example critical theory. A complaint often voiced by critical theorists against constructivism is that the latter focuses too much on a critique of the method and epistemology of the predominant mainstream approaches in the United States, be this mainstream defined as realist and liberal or as quantitative and rationalist. This focus on how we do political science distracts from the critique of the politics of the mainstream to be found in critical theory.[22] In essence, the complaint is that constructivism is crowding out critical theory in the United States. If constructivism were to remain narrowly defined, this crowding out effect would be minimal, because it would be clear that constructivism and critical theory are distinct approaches. The broader the definition of constructivism, with its focus on social theory, however, the less space for critical theory's focus on politics, because critical theory gets lost within the broader category of constructivism.

---

[21] For a series of arguments in favor, see Monroe 2005.
[22] See, for example, Murphy 2007.

The potential for theory imperialism by constructivism as a brand in disciplinary international relations at present in a sense puts it in a position analogous to that of realism faced with the second (science/ tradition) debate in the 1960s. Constructivism as a descriptor can, by losing sight of its core concepts, become a fixture of the disciplinary mainstream. Or it can remain a much less predominant descriptor, but at the same time one that continues to provide a basis for the observations about international politics that led to its development in the first place.

Overtheorizing

Both the brand dilution and the theory imperialism effects can to some degree be mitigated by scholars simply specifying precisely what it is they are doing, clearly placing themselves in a theoretical and epistemological context. Doing so will make it clear whether a particular piece of research fits into a narrower or broader definition of constructivism, and whether another descriptor might be more applicable. But the degree of mitigation of this problem is limited, because even if the description of theoretical and epistemological underpinning is made clear in the text, label effects still matter. Furthermore, too much emphasis on theory-specification can lead to another problem, overtheorizing.

By overtheorizing I mean the inclusion of long discussions of theory, epistemology, and method in works in which they are not necessary. This manifests itself in articles, chapters, and manuscripts in which there is a lengthy theory section, that either describes new methodological tools, or stakes out very specific grounds in epistemological debates, or makes strong claims about the need for a theory of the sociology of international politics. There is then an empirical section that describes a particular case. This mode of construction of an argument is perfectly reasonable, as long as there is a clear connection between the first section and the second. But there is perhaps more theorizing going on out there under the rubric of constructivism than is made necessary by the demands of the empirics.

One might respond that empirical work needs to be grounded in a solid theoretical structure, that epistemological and methodological assumptions need to be made clear, and that all social science has an ontology that should be confronted directly rather than assumed implicitly.[23] This is true up to a certain point, but not beyond it. There is an analogy in quantitative studies of international relations. The way one reads a particular quantitative result may well be impacted by one's epistemology or ontology. For example, a philosophical realist may read a particular correlation between political structure and war in a different way than a logical positivist. But it is often the case that the statistical study itself can be carried out and presented without specifying an ontological intent. The mechanical process of regression analysis is the same either way.

Similarly, a case study looking at the co-constitution of a particular set of agents and structures in international politics need not always take sides in the debate between thick and thin constructivism. Where one places oneself in this epistemological debate may well affect how one reads the case. But that does not necessarily mean that it need affect how one writes the case, or even how one conducts the case study. If one focuses on discourse, the discourse is the same whether or not one sees norms underlying it. If one focuses on norms, one accesses those norms, ultimately, through discursive evidence, which can be read in its own terms. An extensive discussion by the author of her or his views on these debates, therefore, may have little effect on the way in which the reader interprets the empirical evidence.

An example of this point can be found in a recent forum on constructivist methods in international relations edited by Audie Klotz. In this forum, Jeffrey Checkel makes the case for a positivist constructivist method, and Kevin Dunn for a postmodern one. Klotz and Cecelia Lynch argue that, despite differences in epistemology, the differences in method between these two approaches are in fact quite modest.[24] Checkel and Dunn look to different sources of information, because they are asking different questions about different cases. But both ultimately rely on concepts of reasonableness in their decisions about sources of information, sufficiency of information, and suchlike things. Klotz and Lynch make a similar argument at greater length in *Strategies for Research in Constructivist International Relations.*[25]

Three factors that may contribute to the tendency to overtheorize are big-tent definitions of approaches to the study of international

---

[23] On the latter point, see Wendt 1999 and Wight 2006.
[24] Checkel 2006; Dunn 2006; Klotz 2006; and Klotz and Lynch 2006.
[25] Klotz and Lynch 2007.

relations, a tendency within the pedagogy of constructivism toward social theorizing, and an incentive structure in the discipline that favors grand theory. The big-tent (and to a lesser extent the expansive) approach to definition has the effect of diluting the content of descriptive terms. When a fairly restrictive definition of a term like constructivism is generally accepted, then the term by itself can be used as a shorthand for describing the epistemological and methodological context of a specific piece of research. But the broader the definition, the less effective it is to use the term in this shorthand way. With a big-tent definition, in which the term is used to describe membership in a self-selected community rather than a particular aspect of political or social theory, the effectiveness of the term as a research shorthand almost entirely disappears. This leaves the researcher with a need to describe the theoretical, epistemological, and methodological underpinnings of the research more or less from scratch. But if, as Klotz and Lynch argue,[26] there is a common set of methodological tools that constructivists can agree on, and if it is unnecessary to engage in broader epistemological debates to use those tools in the context of specific empirical cases, then these descriptions may often be distracting from rather than contributing to the value of the case study.

A second contributing factor to the tendency to overtheorize may be found in the way we are taught to think about constructivism. Disciplinary pedagogy, the way we teach graduate students, tends to emphasize social theorizing over case work in the teaching of sociological approaches to the study of international relations (in those doctoral programs that teach sociological approaches, that is[27]). The constructivist works that most consistently appear on IR theory syllabi are those that set out the social theory underpinning constructivism, rather than case studies that apply it.[28] Focusing on these works certainly makes sense as pedagogy – understanding the underpinnings of the approach is more important for disciplinary preparation than, say, understanding foreign policy discourse in Canada. But it may be that the lesson that many students take away from these syllabi is that what constructivists do is theorize.

[26] Klotz and Lynch 2006 and 2007.
[27] On which, see Schwartz-Shea 2005.
[28] This claim is based on an admittedly unscientific survey of the international relations field surveys of several leading political science doctoral programs, notably those that posted their syllabi online.

The effects of this emphasis on pedagogy and theorizing are exacerbated by the relationship between constructivism and critical theory. As noted in Chapter 5, these two approaches are often taught as closely related. And in some ways they are, particularly when contrasted with, say, the quantitative mainstream. But teaching them as closely related can mask key differences, such as those discussed in Chapters 4 and 5 relating to the different uses of theory in the two approaches. Conflating critical approaches, with their assumption that social theory cannot be separated from empirics and their emphasis on the emancipatory role of theorizing, with constructivism and its more empiricist starting point, can lead to a greater emphasis on social theorizing in empirical constructivist work where it is not necessary.

A third contributing factor to the tendency to overtheorize in constructivist research applies more broadly to the discipline of international relations, particularly in the United States. This factor is a professional incentive structure that privileges generalizable theory over case studies. The tendency is for more prestigious journals, in their review processes, for example, to privilege articles with conclusions that can be generalized, rather than conclusions that apply only to a specific case.[29] There is therefore an incentive for scholars, whatever their methodology, to claim generalizable conclusions. Furthermore, the more general an article or book, the more likely it is to be widely cited, because it applies in a broader set of circumstances. This is particularly true of grand theory. To the extent that citation is used as a marker in the discipline for success,[30] there is an incentive to theorize, whether or not it is appropriate to the case material being studied.

One of the potential effects of overtheorizing in the context of constructivism that is most problematic is that it can lead to claims of generalizable conclusions that are not in keeping with the historical

[29] For example, *International Organization*'s "Guidelines for Contributors" note that "*IO* features articles that contribute to the improvement of general knowledge ... Although we may publish a manuscript designed to propose a solution to a current world problem, we prefer to publish those that also apply theoretical ideas and findings or address general questions debated in scholarly publications." Viewed at http://assets.cambridge.org/INO/INO_ifc.pdf.

[30] See, for example, Masuoka, Grofman, and Feld 2007, in which the authors, publishing in the professional journal of the American Political Science Association, rank the top 400 scholars in the profession, rated solely by citation count.

contingency that is a key element of the approach. Constructivist logic is incompatible with transhistorical claims about the discursive or normative content of social structures. As such, any claim that agents and norms necessarily interact in a specific way, or that agents respond to and recreate discourses in a particular way, is suspect. Similarly, claims that processes in international politics necessarily follow a particular course are suspect. To argue, then, that a particular process can be identified historically is, in constructivist terms, reasonable. To claim that the pattern, having been found in some instances, is worth looking for in others, is similarly reasonable. But to try to create a broader theory of constructivist political process is not. It defies a core tenet of constructivist logic, which is that agents can recreate social structure in ways that we cannot predict.

Take as an example the concept of norm cascades, following the discussion in Chapter 7. This can be read in three ways. The first is that norms *can* diffuse in a certain pattern, described as a norm cascade, and that this pattern can be identified in specific historical instances. Such a reading of the concept is not at all problematic from a constructivist perspective. It can be read as a model through which to analyze norm diffusion. In this reading, the concept is tautological – an idea that begins subjectively, in the head of an agentive actor, necessarily goes through a cascade if it is to become an intersubjective norm. This reading is also non-problematic, to the extent that the model adds to our understanding of norm diffusion processes. A third reading is that norm cascades involve specific processes of diffusion, and that these processes occur in predictable ways. This reading is, in effect, a grand theory of norm diffusion. And grand theory does not fit well with constructivism's historically contingent ontology.

A key impetus to constructivist grand theorizing can be found in the same disciplinary incentives discussed above – it is often the grand theorists who do best in the profession. And herein lies a problem for ambitious constructivists. The internal logic of constructivism is not particularly suitable for extrapolating from historically contingent cases to grand theory. This limitation can be overcome if the case in question is sufficiently central to contemporary international politics. An example here can be found in John Ruggie's concept of embedded liberalism.[31] It describes one case, but that case helps to explain

---

[31] Ruggie 1982.

the structure of the international political economy for almost half a century. But most cases, or even sets of cases, that constructivists might work on will not have as wide an audience. Alternatively, the disciplinarily ambitious constructivist could focus on grand social theory rather than grand theories of international relations, theory about constructivism rather than theory about politics.[32] But ultimately, too much social theorizing distracts from the constructivist project of the empirical study of co-constitution of agent and structure.

Conclusion

The discussion in this chapter argues for a very constrained constructivism. If the term "constructivism" is to provide us with any specific information about the approach to the study of international relations being taken by a particular work, we must avoid defining it as a residual category, and we must define it in a way that leaves it distinct from the straightforward historical case study. This can be done by defining it in a way that focuses on its core concepts, and those concepts are intersubjectivity and co-constitution. The further common usage of the term within the discipline of international relations gets from these core concepts, the less meaning the term has. Teaching constructivism as anything that does not fit in with mainstream liberalism and realism is not only misleading, but has the effect of further marginalizing approaches that do not fit in well with mainstream constructivism. Recreating social theory arguments anew for each new constructivist case study is unnecessary, distracting, and quite often a waste of time for graduate students and junior scholars whose comparative advantage may be in the case material, but who come to feel that their case work will not be appreciated unless accompanied by a detour into dense social theorizing. And grand theorizing, extrapolating from case studies to general conclusions about how international politics work, can undermine both the ontology and epistemology underlying the constructivist approach.

What then is left to constructivism? Empirical research that directly addresses processes of the co-constitution of structure and agent. Such

---

[32] Wendt 1999 notes the irony of writing a theoretical book about the need for an empirically grounded approach, an irony that will no doubt be clear to readers of this book as well.

research is not limited to work that focuses primarily on the process of co-constitution – it can include research that focuses primarily on the role of structure in constituting agents, or agents in constituting and reconstituting structure. But it is limited to work that allows scope for construction at both ends of the dialectic. Which is to say, it is limited to work that does not assume that either structure or the nature of human agency is fixed. Work that focuses on the interplay of agency and the structure of ideas, the way in which ideas delimit agency while at the same time agency both recreates and changes the structure of intersubjectively accepted ideas. In other words, as opposed to the linear interests-lead-to-outcomes logic (whether those interests are material or ideal) of rationalist theory, constructivism defined narrowly is inherently dialectical.

The intent here is not to argue against the traditional case study, or the explanation of particular political outcomes in terms of strategic logic, or holding agency or structure constant to look at the other. Rather, it is to carve out a space in which the term "constructivism" can refer to an approach to the study of international relations that is distinct, that does not claim to be the only useful approach to such study, but that does offer a contribution that other approaches cannot.

10 | *Constructivism and realism*

Both constructivism and realism often suffer from a castle syndrome, in which they are seen as paradigms, as exclusive and self-contained research orientations for the study of international relations. This syndrome is characterized by definitional overstretch, in which both terms are defined broadly enough, and in a wide enough variety of ways, that they threaten to become meaningless as descriptions of specific approaches to the study of international relations. Furthermore, this overstretch can lead to sets of practices within the rubric of each approach that are internally mutually contradictory. Ironically, this overstretch also leads to arguments that constructivism and realism are incompatible.

This book set out to address these problems. It set out to rehabilitate both constructivism and realism as viable terms of description of specific, internally consistent approaches to the study of international relations, and to discuss their relationship with each other. The various strands of argument presented here may at times seem diffuse, but they coalesce into two primary, and related, sets of arguments. The first of these is that we should define approaches to the study of international relations by their core concepts, and look at the complex ways in which these concepts interact. The second is that having done so with two such approaches, constructivism and realism, we may find that they have more to say to each other than is often assumed.

Within each of these sets are several specific arguments. The first section of this concluding chapter disaggregates the first set of arguments, about core definitions. It looks at the concept of core definitions, and the core definitions suggested here for constructivism and realism. It discusses the effects of a focus on core definitions on the geography of international relations theory, arguing that we should view this geography as a complex matrix rather than as a simple field of castles, and that a focus on core definitions can lead to a call for methodological pluralism. The second section does the same for the

154

second set of arguments, about the relationship between constructivist and realist logic. It looks at both the compatibilities and differences across these logics, and discusses what these two approaches have to offer each other.

Definitions and international relations theory

To this point I have discussed the advantages of narrower, concept-driven definitions of approaches to the study of international relations primarily in terms of internal coherence, and to a lesser extent in terms of disciplinary politics. More specific definitions have the advantage of conveying more information about what a scholar is doing, make sense in their own terms, and are less likely to yield territorial debates about who holds what ground within the academic profession of international relations. These observations are particularly true in the context of the discipline as it is currently constructed in the United States, because both constructivism and realism as discourses have expanded well beyond any viable core concept, and have done so at the expense of meaning, both internal to each discourse and externally, in the relationship between each discourse and the field more broadly.

The argument in favor of narrower definitions is thus more than just an issue of semantics. It is about using terms that have come to be central to the discipline in ways that make conceptual sense. And it is also about creating a conceptual geography of the discipline that makes analytical sense. Three things about this conceptual geography are worth noting. The first is that it is much less simple that the linear, tripartite, or quadripartite conceptual geographies that one often sees in introductory textbooks, because it is much less simplistic. The second is that it is much less prone to disciplinary imperialism than these more simplistic geographies. And the third, a corollary of the second, is that it is much more sympathetic to the idea of pluralism, whether methodological or epistemological, in the study of politics.

The key difference between the more and less simplistic conceptual geographies is that the former tend to be unidimensional, or at most to have two dimensions. But when we speak of international relations theory, we are speaking of arguments made about things as varied as political worldview, morality, method, and ontology. A unidimensional categorization is inevitably going to lose most of the

distinctions among these theories. The number of dimensions needed
to do justice to these distinctions is in fact not finite, in the sense
of not being clearly bounded. A conceptual way of defining specific
approaches yields a conceptual way of thinking about the dimensions or axes on which these approaches differ. I discuss these ideas
about disciplinary geography at greater length below. But first, a brief
review of the way in which this kind of definition helps to rehabilitate
both constructivist and realist logic from the internal contradictions
that accrete as definitions expand.

Constructivism

Constructivists look at ideas, at logics of appropriateness, at rules,
at norms, at discourses. But none of these things is definitional of
constructivism. They are not unique to constructivism, and constructivism need not focus on any particular one of them. To use them
as definitional elements is to mischaracterize the approach. It is also
to necessarily confuse the relationship between constructivist logic
and that of other approaches. Constructivism as a specific logic of
the study of international relations is about the social, which is to
say the intersubjective, construction of international politics. From
this definition follows the focus on the co-constitution of agent and
structure, because only through a recognition of co-constitution can
the researcher address both the social aspect (existent norms and
discourses matter) and the constructed aspect (it is agency, rather
than, say, system structure or biology that create those norms and
discourses). Other features of constructivism also flow from this definition, including the assumption of historical contingency, and a need
for reflexivity on the part of the researcher.

Defining constructivism in this way makes it clearer that constructivist logic is social, rather than political, theory, and therefore that
understanding it in direct opposition to theories of politics, like realism, or liberalism, or Marxism, is misplaced. Defining it in this way
pre-empts fruitless debates about precisely what does or does not constitute materialism. Doing so also obviates attempts to try to distinguish between logics of consequences and of appropriateness, when
human activity can well be both at the same time. And it draws a clear
line between constructivist intersubjectivity, and the purely subjective
understandings of agency to be found in cognitive and psychological

approaches to the study of international relations. Note that I am not arguing here in favor of constructivism over approaches that look at the biology of the brain. Rather, I am simply noting that they are logically, and ontologically, distinct.

Defining constructivism in this way also addresses tensions between thick and thin constructivism, between postmodern and scientifically realist understandings of social constructions. While at the level of general epistemology and ontology the differences between these views of what constitutes social science are substantial, at the level of empirical research the differences can be surprisingly minor. At the same time, a focus on processes of co-constitution rather than emancipation grounds constructivism as an empirical approach that makes it more distinct from critical theory than is often portrayed.

Finally, defining constructivism in terms of intersubjectivity undermines any potential conceit that international politics can be adequately described entirely in terms of this one approach. In pointing out that constructivism does require assumptions about human nature (the assumption of sociability), this definition makes clear that the approach cannot avoid the tension between social construction and human nature. In requiring a certain reflexivity, it points both to a need for normative approaches of politics to complement empirical approaches, and to the need for critical approaches as reflexive check.

Realism

Like constructivism, realism has suffered over the years both from definitional expansion and from theory imperialism. As a result, it can be taken to mean a wide variety of things, and can even be defined as being precisely the opposite of what the classical realists of the mid-twentieth century argued. But even beyond all the problems of expansive definitions that confront constructivism, realism in many of its contemporary forms suffers from a clear internal contradiction, one that can only be resolved by returning to the core concept of classical realism for definition.

That realism has come to be defined by some scholars in ways that are incompatible with the arguments of classical realism is indicative of this internal contradiction, which is between the demands of a prescriptive theory of foreign policy on the one hand and a predictive systems theory on the other. Resolving this contradiction in favor of systems theory loses the core insights of classical realism, and yields a predictive theory that neither addresses the core concept of classical realism, power politics, in a meaningful way, nor succeeds particularly well in explaining international politics. Resolving the contradiction in favor of foreign policy prescription, however, creates an approach that is much more limited in scope, but much more successful within that scope.

Taking power politics seriously as the core concept of realist logic, therefore, means returning realism to its roots as a theory of foreign policy. Losing its claim as an objective scientific theory of international relations allows a rehabilitation of realism as a theory about the reality of power in politics. Doing so also clarifies the relationship between realist logic and normative theory. This relationship has become pointedly recursive and tautological in some contemporary variants of realism, particularly offensive realism, with its argument that states do power-maximize therefore states should power-maximize because that is what states do, an argument that at the same time creates the world that it predicts, and avoids any meaningful discussion of why states should be power-maximizing in the first place. A rehabilitated realist logic makes clearer the relationship between normative theory, necessary but not determinative, and empirical theory, necessary for making good foreign policy but by itself insufficient.

At the same time, returning realism to its foreign policy roots means giving up attempts to systematically predict outcomes. Taking power seriously means taking agency seriously, and taking agency seriously means specifically that we cannot accurately predict the outcomes of foreign policies. This argument, that political outcomes are contingent, is at the root of classical realism's emphasis on prudence in foreign policy, and its prescription that states should marshal their power resources carefully – it is specifically because states cannot accurately predict outcomes that they must be prudent in their uses of power.

Multidimensionality

Defining approaches to the study of international relations by their core concepts makes it clear that these approaches do not lie in a simple linear relationship with each other. They do not, in other words, all vary along the same dimension. Particular pairs of approaches do of course relate to each other in particular ways. For example, classical realism and those approaches to liberalism that posit that some institutional types ameliorate conflict more than others clearly differ along the dimension of whether or not international politics is perfectible. Most students of international politics would likely place themselves on this dimension at some point between the two poles of the pure realist answer and the pure liberal answer, accepting that social institutions are not perfectible, but that some are more effective than others (this dimension is the terrain of the first great debate in international relations theory, between realism and liberalism/idealism/utopianism). As such, presenting a clear opposition between realism and liberalism is a reasonable and useful pedagogical and analytic tool, to the extent that the opposition presented concerns the perfectibility of social institutions.[1]

But once other approaches are added to the mix, the relationships become multidimensional, and thus more complicated. Normative liberal theory, for example, does not fit into the perfectibility-of-institutions dimension at all. Constructivist logic fits into this dimension in complicated ways – it is not compatible with the pure liberal position on institutions, but need not be at the realist end either, for reasons that will be discussed below. When constructivism is contrasted with realism and liberalism in textbooks, however, it is usually for reasons of methodology that have little to do with the core concepts of the latter two approaches. Constructivism is, to a significant degree, orthogonal to realism and liberalism. While there are certainly axes of comparison beyond that of the perfectibility of institutions connecting specific pairs of approaches (such as that from epistemological objectivity to subjectivity on which critical and positivist approaches are opposed), by and large the relationships among most approaches to the study of international relations on most axes are orthogonal.

While discussions of particular sets of axes can prove useful,[2] attempting to enumerate all these axes would be a mistake. This is the case not only because as an exercise it would be way beyond the scope

---

[1] For a similar argument (but one that speaks of ideal types rather than core concepts), see Jackson and Nexon 2009. Their identification of the realism/liberalism dimension is compatible with mine, but their definition of constructivism in opposition to the constraint of anarchy is more permissive than mine.

[2] For example Jackson and Nexon 2009.

of this book, but primarily because there is no clear, easily specified number of dimensions on which approaches to the study of international relations vary. And it is in the recognition of the complexity of this dimensionality that we can avoid the paradigmatic pull to view approaches as mutually exclusive. Specific dimensions are relevant to relationships among specific sets of approaches. The dimensions relevant to the relationship between constructivism and realism are discussed in the second half of this chapter. Various other dimensions have been also been discussed in the various arguments in this book, though, that bear noting.

Some of these link constructivism, and its grounding in a logic of the social, with approaches that are grounded in a logic of the individual. This latter group falls primarily into two general categories, approaches associated with liberalism and those associated with political psychology and cognition. With the latter group, the dimension in question is the extent to which human political activity is determined by biology or social context. As with the perfectibility-of-institutions dimension, most scholars of international relations would probably put themselves somewhere between the two poles of pure individualism and pure social construction. This leaves considerable ground for fruitful interaction between constructivist analyses and those grounded in political psychology and cognition. At the same time, however, it suggests that on this dimension the approaches remain distinct, that attempting to bring the political psychology and cognition research traditions within constructivism, as seems to be a current trend, is misleading and distracts from the useful tension along this dimension.

The relationship between constructivism and approaches associated with liberalism is much more complex, because there is so much variation, along so many dimensions, within liberalism. One of the relationships most often discussed in this context, however, between rationalist variants of liberalism and constructivism, that between consequences and appropriateness, is a red herring. Reduced *ad absurdum*, the logics of both consequences and appropriateness are tautological, leaving no middle ground. Looked at more reasonably, there is a question of the extent to which people act primarily consequentially or appropriately, although distinguishing the two empirically is problematic. But this dimension is not strictly speaking one that links constructivism and rational-choice variants of liberalism, because it is in no way inherent to constructivism to assume that agents do not act strategically.

More broadly, constructivist methodology is compatible with a normatively liberal research program, but less so with a predictively liberal one. In the latter case, the dimension of difference is the same as that between liberalism and realism, that of the perfectibility of social institutions. Those liberal approaches, ranging from rational choice theory to Wilsonian liberalism, that predict that individuals will respond to institutions in a particular way, are incompatible with the constructivist assumptions concerning both human agency and historical contingency. In the former case, a normatively liberal agenda can inform the choice of social constructions studied, and constructivist research can inform liberal policy prescriptions by clarifying the nature of existing institutions, and thereby providing information useful in the recreation of those institutions in a more liberal fashion. In this, constructivist logic is neither more nor less compatible with liberalism than with any other normative approach to the study of international relations. The dimension linking normative liberalism with constructivism is that connecting the empirical with the normative, similar to the dimension linking normative liberalism with realism.

The other set of links that bear noting are those relating to the logic of the social more generally. There are several aspects to this logic that link different approaches to the study of international relations in different ways. One of these relates to a dimension noted above, the extent to which human political activity is determined by biology or social context. On a closely related dimension is the question of how we deal with human nature, whether by induction (questioning it empirically) or deduction (assuming it). Liberal approaches differ amongst themselves; rationalism assumes a particular human nature, while normative liberalism is not necessarily linked to either end of the spectrum. Constructivism is like rationalism in this sense in that it assumes a particular human nature, one that is at the same time sociable and highly malleable. Realism, on the other hand, need not be associated with particular assumptions about human nature, and in this sense has a greater affinity with approaches such as political psychology and cognition than does constructivism.

Another aspect of the logic of the social is the dimension of social agency, and, as a corollary, social policy. This is a dimension that

distinguishes among realism and constructivism at one end of the
dimensional spectrum, and critical approaches at the other. It has
been noted that some of the seminal realist theorists, particularly
E. H. Carr, end up sounding somewhat like critical theorists, because
their recognition that the combination of moral relativism and the
role of power politics as empirical observations can lead to any moral
claims being interpreted by others as the use of power.[3] In this sense
any realism that takes the idea of power politics seriously does have
an affinity with critical approaches, an affinity that is entirely compatible with constructivism's emphasis on the historical contingency
of social institutions.

But this affinity is limited by differences between realism and constructivism on the one hand and critical approaches on the other with
respect to the logic of the social. For critical theory the idea of a
social good, a necessary underpinning of social policy prescription,
is problematic – social structures, and the power inherent in them,
constrain the individual, and the prescriptive aspects of critical theory
therefore tend to focus on the idea of individual emancipation. The
idea of social policy, of social emancipation, is problematic because
the social result remains a power structure, which demands a contin-
ued emphasis on emancipation. But for realism, the social good (in the
form of the national interest) is the point – it is what realism is there to
promote and defend. Constructivist logic does not look at the social
good in the same prescriptive way as realist (and particularly classical
realist) logic, but sees it as a social construction, as intersubjective. As
such, it is nonetheless at the same end of the spectrum on this issue
as realism.

Pluralism

All of this suggests that various approaches to the study of international relations relate to each other in various different ways, each
having affinities with some approaches on some dimensions and with
others on other dimensions. They cannot reasonably be lined up and
compared as if one dimension were sufficient, nor understood as self-
contained and mutually exclusive paradigms each of which is, for its
practitioners, sufficient unto itself for a complete understanding of

---

[3] See, for example, Kubálková 1998.

international politics. The various approaches are simply not directly comparable. Some are based on political assumptions, others on epistemological or ontological assumptions, while yet others are built around methodologies or specific political questions.

This observation lends itself to two conclusions, one about the pedagogy of international relations, and the other about research. The pedagogical conclusion is that teaching international relations either as a set of separate paradigmatic castles (the realism/liberalism/constructivsm model), or as arrayed on a linear scale of some sort (such as a positivism/post-positivism line with statistics on one end and deconstruction on the other) is problematic. While teaching international relations requires simplifying the range of approaches on offer, simplifying into one dimension is perhaps going too far, sacrificing too much of the richness of the field. As a pedagogical tool, teaching even two or three of the dimensions across which approaches to international relations vary is a vast improvement over teaching just one, because it suggests multidimensionality in a way that teaching just one cannot. It shows that different approaches vary in different ways, a point lost in any unidimensional pedagogy.

This is true both at the undergraduate level, where method is often taught as politics, and at the graduate level, where politics is often taught as method. At the undergraduate level, the creation of the realist/liberal/constructivist trifecta means that constructivism is lumped in with two theories of politics. As such, students are primed to see constructivism as a theory of politics, which it is not, rather than as social theory (this is even more true when Marxism is included as a fourth paradigm). At the graduate level, conversely, the focus on method and methodology means that students are primed to see the discipline in terms of method, rather than in terms of politics. Whether the focus is on politics or method, the complex relationships of approaches on different dimensions is lost.

The conclusion about research into international relations is that pluralism is desirable not only in general across the field, but often within the context of specific approaches. There are two arguments in favor of such an internal pluralism. The first is that specific approaches focus on specific aspects of the study of international relations, aspects that are more often than not orthogonal to those around which other approaches are focused. This means that any given approach is unlikely to be by itself a sufficient basis for research. Realism, for example, can be understood as a theory of the imperfectability of political institutions. This theory may not be compatible with all social science methodologies, but by the same token it is not limited to one such methodology. Similarly, constructivism as social theory does not imply any particular theory of politics. As such, the various approaches to the study of international relations need to be combined with others if they are to be of use in the context of a specific research program. The researcher may have a commitment to a set of approaches that, when combined, provide the range of intellectual tools needed to study a particular research question. But if this commitment is exclusive, that researcher will be quite limited in the range of questions that he or she can address.

Each approach, focused as it is on a specific aspect of the study of international relations, is also limited by its focus. An approach is most useful when this aspect is central to a particular research question. The less central the particular aspect is to a particular research question, the less useful the approach is. A dedicated constructivist, for example, is likely to believe that understanding the co-construction of agent and structure is necessary to an understanding of international politics. But few constructivists are likely to believe that agents are entirely created by social structures, that they are a *tabula rasa* on which society can write any set of identities and interests whatsoever. In fact, to believe so would be self-contradictory, in that such a *tabula rasa* would leave no room for agency, and therefore no basis for change in structure. Recognizing this contradiction leaves the constructivist two options. The first is what I called theory imperialism in the last chapter, redefining constructivism in such a way that specifically agency-focused approaches, such as political psychology and cognition, can be brought within it. But doing so means losing the core concept of constructivism. The second is a recognition that some questions are best answered using a constructivist approach, and others are best answered using other approaches. Understanding constructivism to be a paradigm suggests choosing the first of these options. Understanding it as a specific logic suggests the second.

The same argument can be made for realism. On the one hand, a core premise of classical realism is that social institutions are imperfectible. On the other hand, few realists would argue that some institutions are not to be preferred to others. In situations in which the core security of the state is not in question, most realists would accept that approaches other than realism are needed to understand and prescribe behavior. Even at their most polemical, realists are more likely to insist only that low politics are less important and less interesting than high politics, rather than arguing that low politics are entirely irrelevant.[4]

The second reason that a multidimensional understanding of the relationships among approaches to the study of international relations argues in favor of pluralism is that on many of these dimensions, approaches exist in dialectical relationship to each other, rather than in simple opposition. To use such an approach well, to arrive at a synthetic understanding of international politics, therefore, requires that one recognize its antithesis. This sort of dialectic is clearest in the relationship between realism and idealism, as E. H. Carr argued explicitly.[5] It is also present in the relationship between both constructivism and realism on the one hand, and critical theory on the other, inasmuch as any approach to the study of social science that is reflexive needs intellectual tools with which to examine the effects of its concepts on that which it studies, and critical theory provides those tools. Other instances exist as well, beyond the realm of issues that this book has focused on. For example, proponents of both deductive and inductive approaches to social science generally recognize that the actual practice of the study of social science is a synthesis of both, and those who do not recognize this are on shaky epistemological ground.

Constructivism and realism

This discussion of definitions and international relations theory brings us at last to the core relationship in this book, that between constructivism and realism. That the two approaches are not mutually incompatible has already been belabored. But how compatible are they? What would a marriage of the two produce, and what would its potential and limitations be? Several examples of research that might be called realist–constructivist (although they do not all self-identify as such) can already be found in the international relations

---

[4] An example of realists at their most polemical can be found in Mearsheimer 1994/1995.
[5] Carr 1964.

literature, ranging from studies of the role of ideas in the making of grand strategy, to the coercive use of language and soft power, to the creation of security threats.[6] I do not propose here to favor one or another specific realist–constructivist approach, but rather suggest a set of thoughts on research that usefully draws on the core concepts of both constructivism and realism, and that embraces all of these existing examples. These thoughts highlight both the possibilities of this combination, and its limitations.

I do not argue that constructivism should be realist, or that realism should be constructivist – to do either would be to contradict the call to pluralism discussed above. In this sense, the argument being made here is distinct from some recent work that suggests either that realism is inherently constructivist, or that constructivism is inherently realist.[7] Rather, I argue that there are grounds for overlap between the two.[8] Constructivism and realism have clear compatibilities, but also clear differences. This means that each can reinforce, but not be subsumed by, the other. The first part of this section examines these compatibilities and differences. The second part looks at what each approach has to offer the other.

Compatibilities and differences

Three key compatibilities between constructivist and realist logic have been explored in this book. These are a grounding in the logic of the social, a recognition of historical contingency, and a need for reflexivity. All three are elements of classical realism that were lost in the second great debate, and in the transition from classical realism to neorealism. And all three are elements that need to be restored to realism if it is to be able to take power politics seriously as a social phenomenon, provide effective foreign policy prescription, and address issues of change as well as issues of stasis in international politics. It is worth noting at this point that this last observation suggests that constructivist criticisms of neorealism[9] hold despite the arguments in this book. Constructivist and realist logic have definite

---

[6] For example Buzan, Waever, and de Wilde 1998; Mattern 2005b; Dueck 2006; Krebs and Jackson 2007; and Goddard 2009.

[7] Williams 2005 and Steele 2007 respectively.

[8] See Sterling-Folker 2002 for a similar argument.

[9] Such as Ruggie 1983; Wendt 1987; and Wendt 1999.

compatibilities; constructivist and neorealist logic, with the latter's asociality, ahistoricity, and lack of reflexivity, have fewer.

These three compatibilities open a space in which research can be both constructivist and realist. The grounding in the logic of the social distinguishes both approaches from those that are grounded in an individualist ontology. The recognition of historical contingency distinguishes both from theories that focus on the transhistorical structure of international politics, which group includes most "neo-" approaches, inasmuch as neo- tends to be used in the discipline as a synonym for structural. And a need for reflexivity separates both from approaches that claim a pure objectivity, that understand science as removed, and removable, from politics.

Along with these compatibilities, however, constructivist and realist logic also have some definite differences. Most obvious is the difference of focus – the core concepts of the two approaches are orthogonal to each other, located not on different ends of a dimension of difference in international relations theory, but on different dimensions altogether. As such, whatever their compatibilities, the two approaches remain distinct. There is no realist constructivism (or constructivist realism) that can replace both approaches as distinct entities. In other words, the difference in focus means that while there is scope for a realist constructivism, there remains a nonrealist constructivism, (a constructivism that is not primarily concerned with power as realists understand it) and a non-constructivist realism (a realism that looks at sources of political activity other than co-constitution).

Related to this difference of conceptual focus is a difference of purpose. As an empirical approach to the study of international relations, constructivism's proximate purpose is to explain, to use the concept of intersubjectivity as a mechanism to better understand what is happening in international politics. Realism's primary purpose is ultimately policy prescription. One should not make too much of this difference. After all, explanation and understanding are clearly related to effective policy. But the difference is nonetheless important, in that some constructivist work may well not be particularly relevant to realist purposes (if it does not relate directly to issues of foreign policy and national interest), and much realist work may well be outside the constructivist purpose of understanding international politics through the lens of co-constitution.

Two other differences are worth mentioning, the first having to do with idealism and the second with power. Constructivism and realism have quite different relationships with idealism, with normative approaches to the study of international relations. For constructivist theory, normative theories (as opposed to theories of norms) are objects of study. Constructivist logic does not call for the privileging of any particular political morality over any other – all are historically contingent social constructs. Constructivist scholars, as is the case with all scholars in the discipline, are no doubt motivated in their research by their own political morality, which is both something that will affect their choice of topic of study, and something of which they need to be reflexively aware. But constructivism *per se* is nonetheless focused on understanding differences in idealisms, rather than on promoting a particular idealism.[10]

Realism, on the other hand, is in a much more direct relationship with idealism. Meaningful foreign policy requires a dialectical relationship between an understanding of power and a commitment not to the concept of political morality in general, but to a specific political morality. In this sense, the demands of reflexivity on realism and constructivism are different. For constructivists, this demand is the recognition that the researcher is likely to be reading others' political morality through the lens of one's own. For realists, it is the recognition that others' political morality is as strongly held, and as legitimate in the eyes of its holders, as one's own. Somewhat counterintuitively, then, good realism requires a more clearly articulated subjective political morality than does good constructivism.

The final difference addressed in this context is different understandings of power. As discussed in various places in this book, realism's concept of power is narrower than constructivism's. Realism's concept of power is broader than is generally credited by its critics, and is in no way crudely material. But realism's policy focus does ultimately demand a relational approach to understanding power – power that can be used in the conduct of policy, rather than power as pure constraint. Constructivism is open to both the relational and the structural understandings of power. Work that focuses on the latter can inform realist analysis, but is not in itself realist, in the same way that critical theories of structural power in international politics can inform, but are distinct from, realism.

[10] Hoffmann 2009.

What they have to offer each other

Constructivism and realism, then, are distinct but compatible approaches. There is scope for both for a realist constructivism and for a constructivist realism, but neither entirely displaces the unmodified approach. A realist constructivism is a constructivism in which a concern for power politics, understood as relational rather than structural, is central. It is also one in which the links to social policy (including, but not limited to, foreign policy) are made clear. A constructivist realism is a realism that takes intersubjectivity and co-constitution seriously, that focuses on social structures as the locus of change in international politics. Whether a particular work is one or the other is a matter of emphasis more than a matter of kind.

That there is scope for combining the two establishes only that it can be done, however, not that anyone should want to do it. The questions remain, then, of what realism has to offer constructivists, and what constructivism has to offer realists.

In response to the first of these questions, realism offers contructivists two things. The first of these is a way to think about power politics that is more comprehensive than that offered by the liberal constructivisms most often found in the United States, yet at the same time more social than that offered by the structural visions of power often found in critical approaches. In the liberal view, power can be effectively constrained by social institutions, and therefore power becomes secondary in focus to institutions. In the critical view, power inheres in those same social institutions, rather than in agency. As such, power is something that one can be emancipated from, but cannot effectively master. Neither approach adequately allows for the study of the use of power by agents to effectively and intentionally reconstitute social structure. For those constructivists who choose to study power as a tool of policy by actors in international politics, be those actors individual or corporate, realism provides the conceptual framework with which to do so in a way that other theories of international politics do not. This is particularly true for those constructivists who study foreign policy.[11]

The second thing that realism offers constructivists is a way to think about the relationship between empirical research and policy,

---

[11] For example Dueck 2006.

including but not limited in this context to foreign policy. The link between constructivist research and policy, however, is by no means straightforward. Once we develop a model of the discursive and normative structures operating in a particular context in international politics, what do we do with it? One possible answer is nothing – understanding is an end in itself. For those scholars for whom this answer is insufficient, who want to affect as well as understand international politics, the question becomes, once we understand social constructions, what do we do about them? To this question in turn there are many answers. Some involve activity on an individual basis to create new or recreate existing constructions. Others involve working through extant social institutions. To the extent that policy goals include state policy with respect to international politics, realism, through the shared mechanism of the logic of the social, provides a useful way of translating understanding into state policy.

One might respond that there are other ways of translating constructivist research and normative commitment into policy, a response that one might expect, for example, from mainstream liberal constructivists in the United States. But liberal constructivism (or for that matter any constructivism motivated by a normative commitment) generates an awkward relationship between a belief that a normative commitment will succeed because of the strength of its own logic, and the ontological commitment to social construction. The former suggests a teleological view of political morality, the latter a contextual view. The policy prescription that flows from the teleological view is that one should simply promote the right set of norms, and they will sooner or later triumph over others in the marketplace of ideas. But the ontology suggests no reason why this should be the case.

A realist constructivism provides a mechanism for addressing the tension between these commitments. Realism cautions us that policy that we make with the best of intentions may well be interpreted by others as power politics couched in the language of political morality. It also cautions us that policy that we make with the best of intentions may well be used by others as a tool to maximize their own power. A realist constructivism is well placed to see that, however much we may believe in a political morality, to see that morality in teleological terms can as a policy matter be counterproductive. It is well placed to see that not only do discursive and normative structures need to be constantly recreated, but that they often must be recreated against opposition, and that to recreate them to reflect a particular political morality can require the application of power as well as reason.[12]

Meanwhile, constructivism can similarly offer realists two things. The first of these is simply a useful way to study politics. Classical realism tells us to study international politics as they are, not as we would like them to be. But that tells what not to do; it tells us little about how to go about studying politics as they are, beyond the admonition that social relations, particularly with respect to governance, are likely to remain political in nature. This absence of method likely contributed to the extent to which realism went awry in the second great debate in the discipline of international relations. Constructivism offers to realists a set of methodological tools, a way of going about the study of international relations, that is well developed in its own right, and that is both ontologically and epistemologically congenial to classical realism. It is not by any means the only set of tools, but one that is particularly useful for addressing questions about social structure and change, questions that are central to realist concerns with the national interest in an evolving yet anarchical world.

This set of tools is one that would likely sound eminently reasonable both to classical and to many neoclassical realists were constructivism not so often presented in the discipline in opposition to realism. In discussing foreign policy prescriptions, and the limits of power implied by their prescriptions, realists often in fact sound constructivist. The classical realist view of politics, with its respect for the limits of force and its recognition of potential for agency in others, is epistemologically more in sympathy with the dialectic, synthetic process of co-constitution highlighted by constructivism than with the linear, cause and effect processes embedded in the "scientific" approach to the study of politics as understood in the second debate. A constructivist realism, in this sense, would be a more methodologically and conceptually rigorous version of what many realists claim already to be doing. In this sense, in other words, it would heed Morgenthau's call for the rational study of international relations[13] in a way that many "scientific" approaches do not. It would help neoclassical realism specifically to get away from its reliance

[12] For example Mattern 2005b; Krebs and Jackson 2007.
[13] Morgenthau 1948.

on a sterile structuralism as a starting point for the study of foreign policy,[14] by providing the tools for examining the normative content of the national interest.

The second thing that constructivism can offer is a way to deal with the tension in realism between both a commitment to a political morality and an acceptance of moral relativism. The commitment to a political morality is driven by the concept of the national interest – without a national interest there is no logic to supporting the aggregation of power by one's state. But the national interest itself demands content beyond power. Realists have dealt with this content in a variety of ways. Morgenthau argued that the national interest was the maintenance of peace.[15] It is easy to see this argument in terms of basic survival when viewed through the lens of the Cold War and mutual assured destruction. But he made this argument long before the era of Mutually Assured Destruction (MAD), before there was even a nuclear confrontation. His argument is in fact one of moral purpose – that large-scale war is bad not because of the threat it poses to national survival, but because of its human cost.

More recently, however, many realists have reified the idea of state survival as the only national interest worthy of note. This view of the national interest is problematic for a variety of reasons. One is that, to the extent that only great powers are in a position to use their power directly to ensure their survival, such a definition of the national interest would limit realism's relevance only to great powers. Another is that national survival is rarely threatened, making a realism focused only on survival irrelevant most of the time. If realists wish to be relevant beyond the very rare instances when the very survival of great powers is at issue, they need a concept of national interest beyond survival. And there is no basis for establishing such an interest without normative content that is held intersubjectively by those in whose name the state acts. Other realists have tacitly accepted the idea of a national interest beyond survival by inducing that interest from state behavior.[16] But the methods used give only a static image of the national interest, and show only the policy outputs of that interest, not the normative concerns driving it. Contemporary realism, then, has fallen into precisely the trap of which Carr warned,

---

[14] Lobell, Ripsman, and Taliaferro 2009.
[15] Morgenthau 1948.   [16] For example Krasner 1978.

that of making power sterile by focusing on it at the expense of social purpose.[17]

In other words, realists have tended over time to deal with the issue of political morality by trying to ignore it, or by trying to induce it. But a realism that is not cognizant of what the national interest is, what the state is trying to accomplish with its foreign policy, will not be able to prescribe effectively. And yet, accepting uncritically a particular political morality underlying the national interest risks leading to precisely to the sort of Wilsonian liberal imposition that provided the foil for both Carr and Morgenthau. Constructivist method, by providing realists with a way to think about political morality that distinguishes clearly between the categories of empirical social construct and normative theory, allows realists to study political moralities comparatively without seeing the specific political morality underlying their own foreign policy prescriptions in a purely relative light. In other words, it provides the social theory needed to bridge the gap in realism between the beliefs underlying foreign policy, and the reality that those beliefs are not universally held.

[17] Carr 1964.

References

Adler, Emanuel 1997. "Seizing the Middle Ground: Constructivism in World Politics," *European Journal of International Relations* 3: 319–363.

Adler, Emanuel and Michael Barnett (eds.) 1998. *Security Communities.* Cambridge: Cambridge University Press.

Althusser, Louis 1971. *Lenin and Philosophy, and Other Essays*, trans. Ben Brewster. New York: Monthly Review Press.

Arendt, Hannah 1958. *The Human Condition.* Chicago: University of Chicago Press.

Arfi, Badredine 2005. "Resolving the Trust Predicament in IR: A Quantum Game-Theoretic Approach," *Theory and Decision* 59: 127–174.

Aristotle 1958. *The Politics of Aristotle*, ed. and trans. Ernest Barker. Oxford: Oxford University Press.

Ashley, Richard 1984. "The Poverty of Neorealism," *International Organization* 38: 225–286.

Ashley, Richard and R.B.J. Walker 1990. "Speaking the Language of Exile: Dissident Thought in International Studies," *International Studies Quarterly* 34: 259–268.

Bachrach, Peter and Morton Baratz 1962. "Two Faces of Power," *American Political Science Review* 56: 947–952.

Baldwin, David 1979. "Power Analysis and World Politics: New Trends Versus Old Tendencies," *World Politics* 31: 161–194.

1989. *Paradoxes of Power.* New York: Blackwell.

Barkin, J. Samuel 1998. "The Evolution of the Constitution of Sovereignty and the Emergence of Human Rights Norms," *Millennium* 27: 229–252.

2003a. "Realist Constructivism," *International Studies Review* 5:3: 325–342.

2003b. *Social Construction and the Logic of Money: Financial Predominance and International Economic Leadership.* Albany: State University of New York Press.

2008. "Qualitative Methods?" In Audie Klotz and Deepa Prakash (eds.), *Qualitative Methods in International Relations: A Pluralist Guide.* New York: Palgrave Macmillan.

Barkin, J. Samuel and Bruce Cronin 1994. "The State and the Nation: Changing Norms and the Rules of Sovereignty in International Relations," *International Organization* 48: 107–130.

Barnett, Michael and Raymond Duvall 2005. "Power in International Politics," *International Organization* 59: 39–75.

Bartelson, Jens 1998. "Second Natures: Is the State Identical With Itself?" *European Journal of International Relations* 4: 295–326.

Bernstein, Steven 2001. *The Compromise of Liberal Environmentalism.* New York: Columbia University Press.

Biebricher, Thomas 2005. "Habermas, Foucault, and Nietzsche: A Double Misunderstanding," *Foucault Studies* 3: 1–26.

Booth, Ken 1991. "Security and Emancipation," *Review of International Studies* 17: 313–326.

Boucoyannis, Deborah 2007. "The International Wanderings of a Liberal Idea, or Why Liberals Can Learn to Stop Worrying and Love the Balance of Power," *Perspectives on Politics* 5: 703–728.

Bourdieu, Pierre 1998. *Practical Reason: On the Theory of Action.* Stanford, CA: Stanford University Press.

Brams, Steven 1980. *Biblical Games: A Strategic Analysis of Stories in the Old Testament.* Cambridge, MA: MIT Press.

Brown, Chris 1994. "Turtles All the Way Down: Anti-Foundationalism, Critical Theory, and International Relations," *Millennium* 23: 213–236.

Bueno de Mesquita, Bruce 1981. *The War Trap.* New Haven, CT: Yale University Press.

1985. "The War Trap Revisited: A Revised Expected Utility Model," *American Political Science Review* 79: 156–177.

Bueno de Mesquita, Bruce, James Morrow, Randolph Siverson, and Alastair Smith 1999. "An Institutional Explanation of the Democratic Peace," *American Political Science Review* 93: 791–807.

Bull, Hedley 1977. *The Anarchical Society: A Study of Order in World Politics.* New York: Columbia University Press.

Burchill, Scott, Richard Devetak, Andrew Linklater, Matthew Paterson, Christian Reus-Smit, and Jacqui True 2001. *Theories of International Relations,* 2nd edition. New York: Palgrave Macmillan.

Burgerman, Susan 2001. *Moral Victories: How Activists Provoke Multilateral Action.* Ithaca, NY: Cornell University Press.

Buzan, Barry, Ole Waever, and Jaap de Wilde 1998. *Security: A New Framework for Analysis.* Boulder, CO: Lynne Rienner.

Campbell, David 1998. *National Deconstruction: Violence, Identity, and Justice in Bosnia.* Minneapolis: University of Minnesota Press.

Carr, E. H. 1964. *The Twenty Years' Crisis, 1919–1939: An Introduction to the Study of International Relations.* Reprinted from the earlier edition. New York: Harper & Row.

Chan, Steve 1997. "In Search of Democratic Peace: Problems and Promise," *Mearshon International Studies Review* 41: 59–91.

Checkel, Jeffrey 2006. "Tracing Causal Mechanisms," *International Studies Review* 8: 362–370.

Chernoff, Fred 2007. "Critical Realism, Scientific Realism, and International Relations Theory," *Millennium* 35: 399–407.

Chwieroth, Jeffrey 2007. "Testing and Measuring the Role of Ideas: The Case of Neoliberalism in the International Monetary Fund," *International Studies Quarterly* 51: 5–30.

Claude, Inis 1962. *Power and International Relations*. New York: Random House.

Copeland, Dale 2000. "The Constructivist Challenge to Structural Realism: A Review Essay," *International Security* 25: 187–212.

  2003. "A Realist Critique of the English School," *Review of International Studies* 29: 427–441.

Cox, Robert 1986. "Social Forces, States, and World Orders: Beyond International Relations Theory." In Robert Keohane (ed.), *Neorealism and its Critics*. New York: Columbia University Press.

  1987. *Production, Power, and World Order: Social Forces and the Making of History*. New York: Columbia University Press.

Cronin, Bruce 1999. *Community Under Anarchy: Transnational Identity and the Evolution of Cooperation*. New York: Columbia University Press.

Dahl, Robert 1961. *Who Governs? Democracy and Power in an American City*. New Haven, CT: Yale University Press.

Der Derian, James 1990. "The (S)pace of International Relations: Simulation, Surveillance, and Speed," *International Studies Quarterly* 34: 295–310.

Dessler, David 1989. "What's at Stake in the Agent-Structure Debate?" *International Organization* 43: 441–473.

Deudney, Daniel 2006. *Bounding Power: Republican Security Theory from the Polis to the Global Village*. Princeton, NJ: Princeton University Press.

Deudney, Daniel and Richard Matthew (eds.) 1999. *Contested Grounds: Security and Conflict in the New Environmental Politics*. Albany: State University of New York Press.

Donnelly, Jack 2000. *Realism and International Relations*. Cambridge: Cambridge University Press.

Doty, Roxanne Lynn 2000. "Desire All the Way Down," *Review of International Studies* 26: 137–139.

Dueck, Colin 2006. *Reluctant Crusaders: Power, Culture, and Change in American Grand Strategy*. Princeton, NJ: Princeton University Press.

Dunn, Kevin 2006. "Examining Historical Representations," *International Studies Review* 8: 370–381.

Dunne, Tim 1998. *Inventing International Society: A History of the English School.* Basingstoke: Macmillan.

Ellis, David 2005. *"Defending the International Interest."* Gainesville, FL: University of Florida Doctoral Dissertation.

2009. "On the Possibility of 'International Community'," *International Studies Review* 11: 1–26.

Elster, Jon 1983. *Sour Grapes: Studies in the Subversion of Rationality.* Cambridge: Cambridge University Press.

1989. *Nuts and Bolts for the Social Sciences.* Cambridge: Cambridge University Press.

Fearon, James 1995. "Rationalist Explanations for War," *International Organization* 49: 379–414.

Fearon, James and Alexander Wendt 2002. "Rationalism versus Constructivism: A Skeptical View." In Walter Carlesnaes, Thomas Risse-Kappen, and Beth Simmons (eds.), *Handbook of International Relations.* London: Sage.

Fierke, Karen and Knud Erik Jørgensen (eds.) 2001. *Constructing International Relations: The Next Generation.* Armonk, NY: M.E. Sharpe.

Finnemore, Martha 1996a. *National Interest in International Society.* Ithaca, NY: Cornell University Press.

1996b. "Norms, Culture, and World Politics: Insights from Sociology's Institutionalism," *International Organization* 50: 325–347.

Finnemore, Martha and Kathryn Sikkink 1998. "International Norm Dynamics and Political Change," *International Organization* 52: 887–917.

Flyvbjerg, Bent 2001. *Making Social Science Matter: Why Social Inquiry Fails and How it Can Succeed Again.* Cambridge: Cambridge University Press.

Freyberg-Inan, Annette 2004. *What Moves Man: The Realist Theory of International Relations and its Judgment of Human Nature.* Albany: State University of New York Press.

Friedman, Jeffrey (ed.) 1995. *The Rational Choice Controversy.* New Haven, CT: Yale University Press.

George, Jim 1989. "International Relations and the Search for Thinking Space: Another View of the Third Debate," *International Studies Quarterly* 33: 269–279.

1994. *Discourses of Global Politics: A Critical (Re)Introduction to International Relations.* New York: Macmillan.

George, Jim and David Campbell 1990. "Patterns of Dissent and the Celebration of Difference: Critical Social Theory and International Relations," *International Studies Quarterly* 34: 269–293.

Geuss, Raymond 2002. "Liberalism and its Discontents," *Political Theory* 30: 320–338.

Giles, Michael and James Garand 2007. "Ranking Political Science Journals: Reputational and Citational Approaches," *PS: Political Science & Politics* 40: 741–751.

Gill, Stephen (ed.) 1993. *Gramsci, Historical Materialism, and International Relations*. Cambridge: Cambridge University Press.

Gilpin, Robert 1981. *War and Change in World Politics*. Cambridge: Cambridge University Press.

Goddard, Stacie 2009. "When Right Makes Might: How Prussia Overturned the European Balance of Power," *International Security* 33: 110–142.

Goddard, Stacie and Daniel Nexon 2005. "Paradigm Lost? Reassessing *Theory of International Politics*," *European Journal of International Relations* 11: 9–61.

Goff, Patricia and Kevin Dunn (eds.) 2004. *Identity and Global Politics: Empirical and Theoretical Elaborations*. New York: Palgrave Macmillan.

Green, Donald and Ian Shapiro 1994. *Pathologies of Rational Choice Theory: A Critique of Applications in Political Science*. New Haven, CT: Yale University Press.

Grieco, Joseph 1997. "Realist International Theory and the Study of World Politics." In Michael Doyle and G. John Ikenberry (eds.), *New Thinking in International Relations Theory*. Boulder, CO: Westview Press.

Gunnell, John 1993. *The Descent of Political Theory: The Genealogy of an American Vocation*. Chicago: University of Chicago Press.

Guzzini, Stefano 1993. "Structural Power: The Limits of Neorealist Power Analysis," *International Organization* 47: 443–478.

　1998. *Realism in International Relations and International Political Economy: The Continuing Story of a Death Foretold*. London: Routledge.

　2000. "A Reconstruction of Constructivism in International Relations," *European Journal of International Relations* 6: 147–182.

　2005. "The Concept of Power: A Constructivist Analysis," *Millennium* 33: 495–522.

Haas, Peter, Robert Keohane, and Marc Levy (eds.) 1993. *Institutions for the Earth: Sources of Effective International Environmental Protection*. Cambridge, MA: MIT Press.

Habermas, Jürgen 1984. *The Theory of Communicative Action*, trans. Thomas McCarthy. Boston: Beacon Press.

　1987. *The Philosophical Discourse of Modernity: Twelve Lectures*, trans. Frederick Lawrence. Cambridge, MA: MIT Press.

1991. *The Structural Transformation of the Public Sphere: An Inquiry into a Category of Bourgeois Society*. Cambridge, MA: MIT Press.

Hacking, Ian 1999. *The Social Construction of What?* Cambridge, MA: Harvard University Press.

Hall, Rodney Bruce 1997. "Moral Authority as a Power Resource," *International Organization* 51: 555–589.

Helleiner, Eric 2003. *The Making of National Money: Territorial Currencies in Historical Perspective*. Ithaca, NY: Cornell University Press.

Hoffmann, Matthew 2005. *Ozone Depletion and Climate Change: Constructing a Global Response*. Albany: State University of New York Press.

2009. "Is Constructivist Ethics an Oxymoron?" *International Studies Review* 11: 231–252.

Holsti, Kalevi 1985. *The Dividing Discipline: Hegemony and Diversity in International Theory*. Boston: Allen & Unwin.

Hopf, Ted 1998. "The Promise of Constructivism in International Relations Theory," *International Security* 23: 171–200.

2002. *Social Construction of International Politics: Identities and Foreign Policies, Moscow, 1955 and 1999*. Ithaca, NY: Cornell University Press.

Houghton, David Patrick 2007. "Reinvigorating the Study of Foreign Policy Decision Making: Toward a Constructivist Approach," *Foreign Policy Analysis* 3: 24–45.

Hughes, Barry 2000. *Continuity and Change in World Politics: Competing Perspectives*, 4th edition. Upper Saddle River, NJ: Prentice Hall.

Jackson, Patrick Thaddeus and Daniel Nexon 2004. "Constructivist Realism or Realist-Constructivism?" *International Studies Review* 6: 337–341.

2009. "Paradigmatic Faults in International Relations Theory," *International Studies Quarterly* 53.

Jacobsen, John Kurt 2003. "Duelling Constructivisms: A Post-mortem on the Ideas Debate in Mainstream IR/IPE," *Review of International Studies* 29: 39–60.

Jervis, Robert 1976. *Perception and Misperception in International Politics*. Princeton, NJ: Princeton University Press.

1978. "Cooperation Under the Security Dilemma," *World Politics* 30: 167–214.

1994. "Hans Morgenthau, Realism, and the Scientific Study of International Politics," *Social Research* 61: 853–876.

1998. "Realism in the Study of World Politics," *International Organization* 52: 971–991.

Johnson Bagby, Laurie 1994. "The Use and Abuse of Thucydides in International Relations," *International Organization* 48: 131–153.

Kahler, Miles 1998. "Rationality in International Relations," *International Organization* 52: 919–941.

Kant, Immanuel 1957. *Perpetual Peace*, ed. Lewis White Beck. New York: Macmillan.

Katzenstein, Peter, Robert Keohane, and Stephen Krasner 1998. "*International Organization* and the Study of World Politics," *International Organization* 52: 645–685.

Keck, Margaret and Kathryn Sikkink 1998. *Activists Beyond Borders: Advocacy Networks in International Politics*. Ithaca, NY: Cornell University Press.

Kegley, Charles 1993. "The Neoidealist Moment in International Studies? Realist Myths and the New International Realities," *International Studies Quarterly* 37: 131–147.

Kegley, Charles and Eugene Wittkopf 2001. *World Politics: Trends and Transformations*, 8th edition. Boston: Bedford/St. Martin's Press.

Keohane, Robert 1984. *After Hegemony: Cooperation and Discord in the World Political Economy*. Princeton, NJ: Princeton University Press.

1988. "International Institutions: Two Approaches," *International Studies Quarterly* 32: 379–396.

1989. *International Institutions and State Power: Essays in International Relations Theory*. Boulder, CO: Westview Press.

Kier, Elizabeth and Jonathan Mercer 1996. "Setting Precedents in Anarchy: Military Intervention and Weapons of Mass Destruction," *International Security* 20: 77–106.

King, Gary, Robert Keohane, and Sidney Verba 1994. *Designing Social Inquiry: Scientific Inference in Qualitative Research*. Princeton, NJ: Princeton University Press.

Kirk, Grayson 1947. *The Study of International Relations in American Colleges and Universities*. New York: Council on Foreign Relations.

Klotz, Audie 1995. *Norms in International Relations: The Struggle Against Apartheid*. Ithaca, NY: Cornell University Press.

2006. "Moving Beyond the Agent-Structure Debate," *International Studies Review* 8: 355.

Klotz, Audie and Cecelia Lynch 2006. "Translating Terminologies," *International Studies Review* 8: 356–362.

2007. *Strategies for Research in Constructivist International Relations*. Armonk, NY: M.E. Sharpe.

Klotz, Audie and Deepa Prakash (eds.) 2008. *Qualitative Methods in International Relations*. New York: Palgrave Macmillan.

Knorr, Klaus and James Rosenau (eds.) 1969. *Contending Approaches to International Politics*. Princeton, NJ: Princeton University Press.

Krasner, Stephen 1976. "State Power and the Structure of International Trade," *World Politics* 28: 317–347.

1978. *Defending the National Interest: Raw Materials Investments and US Foreign Policy.* Princeton, NJ: Princeton University Press.

Kratochwil, Friedrich 1984. "Errors Have Their Advantages," *International Organization* 38: 305–320.

2000. "Constructing a New Orthodoxy? Wendt's *Social Theory of International Politics* and the Constructivist Challenge," *Millennium* 29: 73–101.

Kratochwil, Friedrich and John Gerard Ruggie 1986. "International Organization: A State of the Art on an Art of the State," *International Organization* 40: 753–775.

Krebs, Ronald and Patrick Thaddeus Jackson 2007. "Twisting Tongues and Twisting Arms: The Power of Political Rhetoric," *European Journal of International Relations* 13: 35–66.

Kubálková, Vendulka 1998. "The Twenty Years' Catharsis: E. H. Carr and IR." In Vendulka Kubálková, Nicholas Onuf, and Paul Kowert (eds.), *International Relations in a Constructed World.* Armonk, NY: M. E. Sharpe.

Kubálková, Vendulka, Nicholas Onuf, and Paul Kowert 1998 "Constructing Constructivism." In Vendulka Kubálková, Nicholas Onuf, and Paul Kowert (eds.), *International Relations in a Constructed World.* Armonk, NY: M.E. Sharpe.

Kuhn, Thomas 1970. *The Structure of Scientific Revolutions.* Chicago: University of Chicago Press.

1991. "The Natural and the Human Sciences." In D. Hiley, J. Bohman, and R. Shusterman (eds.), *The Interpretative Turn: Philosophy, Science, Culture.* Ithaca, NY: Cornell University Press.

Kurki, Milja 2007. "Critical Realism and Causal Analysis in International Relations," *Millennium* 35: 361–378.

Lang, Anthony 2002. *Agency and Ethics: The Politics of Military Intervention.* Albany: State University of New York Press.

Lapid, Yosef 1989. "The Third Debate: On the Prospects of International Theory in a Post-Positivist Era," *International Studies Quarterly* 33: 235–254.

Lasswell, Harold 1935. *World Politics and Personal Insecurity.* New York: McGraw-Hill.

Lasswell, Harold and Abraham Kaplan 1950. *Power and Society: A Framework for Political Inquiry.* New Haven, CT: Yale University Press.

Lebow, Richard Ned 2001. "Thucydides the Constructivist," *American Political Science Review* 95: 547–560.

2003. *The Tragic Vision of Politics*. Cambridge: Cambridge University Press.

Legro, Jeffrey 1995. *Cooperation Under Fire: Anglo-German Restraint During World War II*. Ithaca, NY: Cornell University Press.

Legro, Jeffrey and Andrew Moravcsik 1999. "Is Anybody Still a Realist?" *International Security* 24: 5–55.

Lenin, Vladimir Illyich 1969 [1917]. *Imperialism: The Highest Stage of Capitalism*. Moscow: International Publishers.

Lieber, Robert 2001. *No Common Power: Understanding International Relations*. 4th edition. Upper Saddle River, NJ: Prentice Hall.

Linklater, Andrew 1990. *Beyond Realism and Marxism: Critical Theory and International Relations*. London: Macmillan.

1992. "The Question of the Next Stage in International Relations Theory: A Critical-Theoretical Point of View," *Millennium* 21: 77–98.

1997. "The Transformation of Political Community: E.H. Carr, Critical Theory and International Relations," *Review of International Studies* 23: 321–338.

1998. *The Transformation of Political Community: Ethical Foundations of the Post-Westphalian Era*. Columbia: University of South Carolina Press.

2001. "Rationalism." In Scott Burchill, Richard Devetak, Andrew Linklater, Matthew Paterson, Christian Reus-Smit, and Jacqui True, *Theories of International Relations*, 2nd edition. New York: Palgrave Macmillan.

Lobell, Steven, Norrin Ripsman, and Jeffrey Taliaferro (eds.) 2009. *Neoclassical Realism, the State, and Foreign Policy*. Cambridge: Cambridge University Press.

Lynch, Mark 1999. *State Interests and Public Spheres: The International Politics of Jordan's Identity*. New York: Columbia University Press.

Macpherson, C.B. 1962. *The Political Theory of Possessive Individualism: Hobbes to Locke*. Oxford: Oxford University Press.

Maliniak, Daniel, Amy Oakes, Susan Peterson, and Michael Tierney 2007. *The View from the Ivory Tower: TRIP Survey of International Relations Faculty in the United States and Canada*. Williamsburg, VA: The Program on the Theory and Practice of International Relations.

March, James and Johan Olsen 1989. *Rediscovering Institutions: The Organizational Basis of Politics*. New York: Free Press.

1998. "The Institutional Dynamics of International Political Orders," *International Organization* 52: 943–969.

Martin, Lisa and Beth Simmons 1998. "Theories and Empirical Studies of International Institutions," *International Organization* 52: 729–757.

Masuoka, Natalie, Bernard Grofman, and Scott Feld 2007. "The Political Science 400: A 20-Year Update," *PS: Political Science & Politics* 40: 133–145.

Mattern, Janice Bially 2005a. *Ordering International Politics: Identity, Crisis, and Representational Force*. London: Routledge.

2005b. "Why Soft Power Isn't So Soft: Representational Force and the Sociolinguistic Construction of Attraction in World Politics," *Millennium* 33: 583–612.

Mearsheimer, John 1983. *Conventional Deterrence*. Ithaca, NY: Cornell University Press.

1994/1995. "The False Promise of International Institutions," *International Security* 19: 5–49.

2001. *The Tragedy of Great Power Politics*. New York: Norton.

2005. "E. H. Carr vs. Idealism: The Battle Rages On," *International Relations* 19: 139–152.

Mercer, Jonathan 1995. "Anarchy and Identity," *International Organization* 49: 229–252.

Mill, John Stuart 1863. *Utilitarianism*. London: Parker, Son, and Bourne.

Milliken, Jennifer 1999. "The Study of Discourse in International Relations: A Critique of Research and Methods," *European Journal of International Relations* 5: 225–254.

Milner, Helen 1997. *Interests, Institutions, and Information: Domestic Politics and International Relations*. Princeton, NJ: Princeton University Press.

Mitchell, Ronald 1994. "Regime Design Matters: Intentional Oil Pollution and Treaty Compliance," *International Organization* 48: 425–458.

Monroe, Kristen Renwick (ed.) 2005. *Perestroika! The Raucous Rebellion in Political Science*. New Haven, CT: Yale University Press.

Morgenthau, Hans 1946. *Scientific Man Versus Power Politics*. Chicago: University of Chicago Press.

1948. *Politics Among Nations: The Struggle for Power and Peace*. New York: Alfred A. Knopf.

1967. *Politics Among Nations: The Struggle for Power and Peace*, 4th edition. New York: Alfred A. Knopf.

1985. *Politics Among Nations: The Struggle for Power and Peace*, 5th edition. New York: Alfred A. Knopf.

Murphy, Craig 1994. *International Organization and Industrial Change: Global Governance Since 1850*. New York: Oxford University Press.

2001 "Political Consequences of the New Inequality," *International Studies Quarterly* 45: 347–356.

2007. "The Promise of Critical IR, Partially Kept," *Review of International Studies* 33: 117–133.

Murphy, Craig and Douglas Nelson 2001. "International Political Economy: A Tale of Two Hederodoxies," *British Journal of Politics and International Relations* 3: 393–412.

Murray, Alastair 1997. *Reconstructing Realism: Between Power Politics and Cosmopolitan Ethics*. Edinburgh: Edinburgh University Press.

New York Times 2002. "A War With Iraq is *Not* in America's National Interest," paid advertisement, September 26.

Nexon, Daniel 2009. "The Balance of Power in the Balance," *World Politics* 61: 330–359.

Nielson, Daniel and Michael Tierney 2003. "Delegation to International Organizations: Agency Theory and World Bank Environmental Reform," *International Organization* 57: 241–276.

Oborne, Peter 2002. "Who Inspired Thatcher's Most Damaging Remark? Tony Blair's Favourite Guru," *The Spectator*, August 24.

Onuf, Nicholas 1989. *World of Our Making: Rules and Rule in Social Theory and International Relations*. Columbia: University of South Carolina Press.

1998. "Constructivism: A User's Manual." In Vendulka Kubálková, Nicholas Onuf, and Paul Kowert (eds.), *International Relations in a Constructed World*. Armonk, NY: M.E. Sharpe.

Onuf, Nicholas and Frank Klink 1989. "Activity, Authority, Rule," *International Studies Quarterly* 33: 149–174.

Oren, Ido. 2000. "Is Culture Independent of National Security? How America's National Security Concerns Shaped 'Political Culture' Research," *European Journal of International Relations* 6: 543–573.

2006. "Can Political Science Emulate the Natural Sciences? The Problem of Self-Disconfirming Analysis," *Polity* 38: 72–100.

2009. "The Unrealism of Contemporary Realism: The Tension between Realist Theory and Realists' Practice," *Perspectives on Politics* 7: 283–301.

Oren, Ido and Ty Solomon 2008. "WMD: Words of Mass Destruction," paper presented at the annual meeting of the International Studies Association, San Francisco.

Owen, John 1994. "How Liberalism Produces Democratic Peace," *International Security* 19: 87–125.

Oxford University Press 2002. *Shorter Oxford English Dictionary*, 5th edition. Oxford: Oxford University Press.

Patomäki, Heikki and Colin Wight 2000. "After Postpositivism? The Promises of Critical Realism," *International Studies Quarterly* 44: 213–237.

Pettman, Ralph 2000. *Commonsense Constructivism: Or the Making of World Affairs*. Armonk, NY: M. E. Sharpe.

Pichler, Hans-Karl 1998. "The Godfathers of 'Truth': Max Weber and Carl Schmitt in Morgenthau's Theory of Power Politics," *Review of International Studies* 24: 185–200.

Pollack, Mark 1997. "Delegation, Agency, and Agenda-Setting in the European Community," *International Organization* 51: 99–134.

Posen, Barry 1984. *The Sources of Military Doctrine: France, Britain, and Germany between the World Wars*. Ithaca, NY: Cornell University Press.

Price, Richard and Christian Reus-Smit 1998. "Dangerous Liaisons? Critical International Theory and Constructivism," *European Journal of International Relations* 4: 259–294.

Rawls, John 1971. *A Theory of Justice*. Cambridge, MA: Harvard University Press.

Reus-Smit, Christian 1999. *The Moral Purpose of the State: Culture, Social Identity, and Institutional Rationality in International Relations*. Princeton, NJ: Princeton University Press.

    2001a. "Constructivism." In Scott Burchill, Richard Devetak, Andrew Linklater, Matthew Paterson, Christian Reus-Smit, and Jacqui True, *Theories of International Relations*, 2nd edition. New York: Palgrave Macmillan.

    2001b. "The Strange Death of Liberal International Theory," *European Journal of International Law* 12: 573–594.

Risse, Thomas 2000. "'Let's Argue!' Communicative Action in World Politics," *International Organization* 54: 1–39.

Risse, Thomas, Stephen Ropp, and Kathryn Sikkink (eds.) 1999. *The Power of Human Rights: International Norms and Domestic Change*. Cambridge: Cambridge University Press.

Rommen, Hans 1944. "Realism and Utopianism in World Affairs," *Review of Politics* 6: 193–215.

Rosati, Jerel 2000. "The Power of Human Cognition in the Study of World Politics," *International Studies Review* 2: 45–75.

Rose, Gideon 1998. "Neoclassical Realism and Theories of Foreign Policy," *World Politics* 51: 144–172.

Rosecrance, Richard, 2001. "Has Realism Become Cost-Benefit Analysis? A Review Essay," *International Security* 26: 132–154.

Rosenthal, Joel 1991. *Righteous Realists: Political Realism, Responsible Power, and American Culture in the Nuclear Age*. Baton Rouge, LA: Louisiana State University Press.

Ruggie, John Gerard 1982. "International Regimes, Transactions, and Change: Embedded Liberalism in the Postwar Economic Order," *International Organizations* 36: 379–415.

1983. "Continuity and Transformation in the World Polity," *World Politics* 35: 261–285.

1993 (ed.). *Multilateralism Matters: The Theory and Praxis of an Institutional Form.* New York: Columbia University Press.

1998. "What Makes the World Hand Together? Neo-Utilitarianism and the Social Constructivist Challenge," *International Organization* 52: 858–885.

Russett, Bruce 1993. *Grasping the Democratic Peace: Principles for a Post-Cold War World.* Princeton, NJ: Princeton University Press.

Russett, Bruce and John Oneal 2001. *Triangulating Peace: Democracy, Interdependence, and International Organizations.* New York: Norton.

Scheuerman, William 2007a. "Carl Schmitt and Hans Morgenthau: Realism and Beyond." In Michael Williams (ed.), *Realism Reconsidered: The Legacy of Hans J. Morgenthau in International Relations.* Oxford: Oxford University Press.

2007b. "Was Morgenthau a Realist? Revisiting *Scientific Man vs. Power Politics,*" *Constellations* 14: 506–530.

Schmidt, Brian 1998. *The Political Discourse of Anarchy: A Disciplinary History of International Relations.* Albany: State University of New York Press.

Schmitt, Carl 1976. *The Concept of the Political,* trans. George Schwab. New Brunswick, NJ: Rutgers University Press.

Schulz, William 2001. *In Our Own Best Interest: How Defending Human Rights Benefits All Americans.* Boston: Beacon Press.

Schuman, Frederick 1933. *International Politics: An Introduction to the Western State System.* New York: McGraw-Hill.

Schwartz-Shea, Peregrine 2005. "The Graduate Student Experience: 'Hegemony' or Balance in Methodological Training?" In Kristen Renwick Monroe (ed.), *Perestroika! The Raucous Rebellion in Political Science.* New Haven, CT: Yale University Press.

Schweller, Randall 1994. "Bandwagoning for Profit: Bringing the Revisionist State Back in," *International Security* 19: 72–107.

1998. *Deadly Imbalances: Tripolarity and Hitler's Strategy of World Conquest.* New York: Columbia University Press.

2003. "The Progressiveness of Neoclassical Realism." In Colin Elman and Miriam Fendius Elman (eds.), *Progress in International Relations Theory: Appraising the Field.* Cambridge, MA: MIT Press.

Scott, John 2000. "Rational Choice Theory." In Gary Browning, Abigail Halcli, and Frank Webster (eds.), *Understanding Contemporary Society: Theories of the Present.* London: Sage.

Shannon, Vaughn 2000. "Norms are What States Make of Them: The Political Psychology of Norm Violation," *International Studies Quarterly* 44: 293–316.

Sikkink, Kathryn 1993. "Human Rights, Principled Issue-Networks, and Sovereignty in Latin America," *International Organization* 47: 411–441.

Singer, J. David 1990. *Models, Methods, and Progress in World Politics: A Peace Research Odyssey*. Boulder, CO: Westview Press.

Smith, Steve 2000. "Wendt's World," *Review of International Studies* 26: 151–163.

2002. "The United States and the Discipline of International Relations: 'Hegemonic Country, Hegemonic Discipline,'" *International Studies Review* 4: 67–85.

Spegele, Roger 1996. *Political Realism in International Theory*. Cambridge: Cambridge University Press.

Steele, Brent 2007. "Liberal-Idealism: A Constructivist Critique," *International Studies Review* 9: 23–52.

Sterling-Folker, Jennifer 2000. "Competing Paradigms or Birds of a Feather? Constructivism and Neoliberal Institutionalism Compared," *International Studies Quarterly* 44: 97–119.

2002. "Realism and the Constructivist Challenge: Rejecting, Reconstructing, or Rereading," *International Studies Review* 4: 73–97.

2004. "Realist-Constructivism and Morality," *International Studies Review* 6: 341–343.

2006a. "Lamarckian with a Vengeance: Human Nature and American International Relations Theory," *Journal of International Relations and Development* 9: 227–246.

2006b. "Constructivism." In Sterling-Folker (ed.), *Making Sense of International Relations Theory*. Boulder, CO: Lynne Rienner.

2009. "Realist Theorizing as Tradition: Forward Is as Forward Does." In Annette Freyberg-Inan, Patrick James, and Ewan Harrison (eds.), *Rethinking Realism in International Relations: Between Tradition and Innovation*. Baltimore: Johns Hopkins University Press.

Sterling-Folker, Jennifer and Rosemary Shinko 2005. "Discourses of Power: Traversing the Realist-Postmodern Divide," *Millennium: Journal of International Studies* 33: 637–664.

Strange, Susan 1987. "The Persistent Myth of Lost Hegemony," *International Organization* 41: 551–574.

Swedberg, Richard 2005. "Can There Be a Sociological Concept of Interest?" *Theory and Society* 34: 359–390.

Tannenwald, Nina 1999. "The Nuclear Taboo: The United States and the Normative Basis of Nuclear Non-Use," *International Organization* 53: 433–468.

Vasquez, John 1983. *The Power of Power Politics: A Critique*. New Brunswick, NJ: Rutgers University Press.

1998. *The Power of Power Politics: From Classical Realism to Neotraditionalism*. Cambridge: Cambridge University Press.

Waever, Ole 1996. "The Rise and Fall of the Inter-Paradigm Debate." In Steve Smith, Ken Booth, and Marysia Zalewski (eds.), *International Theory: Positivism and Beyond*. Cambridge: Cambridge University Press.

1997. "Figures of International Thought: Introducing Persons Instead of Paradigms." In Iver Neumann and Ole Waever (eds.), *The Future of International Relations: Masters in the Making?* London: Routledge.

Walker, R.B.J. 1987. "Realism, Change, and International Political Theory," *International Studies Quarterly* 31: 65–86.

1993. *Inside/Outside: International Relations as Political Theory*. Cambridge: Cambridge University Press.

Wallerstein, Immanuel 1974. *The Modern World-System: Capitalist Agriculture and the Origins of the European World-Economy in the Sixteenth Century*. New York: Academic Press.

1979. *The Capitalist World-Economy*. New York: Cambridge University Press.

Walt, Stephen 1987. *The Origins of Alliances*. Ithaca, NY: Cornell University Press.

Waltz, Kenneth 1959. *Man, the State, and War*. New York: Columbia University Press.

1967. *Foreign Policy and Democratic Politics: The American and British Experience*. Boston: Little, Brown.

1979. *Theory of International Politics*. Reading, MA: Addison-Wesley.

1986. "Reflections on *Theory of International Politics*: A Response to My Critics." In Robert Keohane (ed.), *Neorealism and its Critics*. New York: Columbia University Press.

Wendt, Alexander 1987. "The Agent-Structure Problem in International Relations Theory," *International Organization* 41: 335–370.

1992. "Anarchy is What States Make of it: The Social Construction of Power Politics," *International Organization* 46: 391–425.

1994. "Collective Identity Formation and the International State," *American Political Science Review* 88: 384–396.

1999. *Social Theory of International Politics*. Cambridge: Cambridge University Press.

2003. "Why a World State is Inevitable," *European Journal of International Relations* 9: 491–542.

Wight, Colin 2006. *Agents, Structures, and International Relations: Politics as Ontology*. Cambridge: Cambridge University Press.

2007. "A Manifesto for Scientific Realism in IR: Assuming the Can-Opener Won't Work!" *Millennium* 35: 379–398.

Wight, Martin 1946. *Power Politics.* London: Royal Institute of International Affairs.

Williams, Michael 2005. *The Realist Tradition and the Limits of International Relations.* Cambridge: Cambridge University Press.

Wolfers, Arnold 1962. *Discord and Collaboration: Essays on International Politics.* Baltimore: Johns Hopkins University Press.

Wyn Jones, Richard (ed.) 2001. *Critical Theory & World Politics.* Boulder, CO: Lynne Rienner.

Zehfuss, Maja 2002. *Constructivism in International Relations: The Politics of Reality.* Cambridge: Cambridge University Press.

Žižek, Slavoj 2000. *The Fragile Absolute – Or, Why is the Christian Legacy Worth Fighting For?* New York: Verso.

Index